WHOLE CHILD EDUCATION

Traditional approaches to education have tended to be piecemeal and to focus on test scores and narrowly defined parameters of performance and achievement. In *Whole Child Education*, John P. Miller offers an alternative model that fosters relationships between various forms of thinking, links body and mind, and recognizes the inner life of the child.

Addressing specific issues related to teaching, the curriculum, the school, and teacher wellness, Miller presents three basic approaches – transmission, transaction, and transformation – that facilitate a connection with the whole student. Practical examples from teachers who have incorporated Miller's ideas into their classrooms and a description of Toronto's Whole Child School (founded in 2009) illustrate how principles of whole child education can be implemented on both a small and large scale. Inspired by the powerful vision of Martin Luther King and his concept of the Beloved Community, *Whole Child Education* is a vehicle for building community through holistic education.

JOHN P. MILLER is a professor in the Department of Curriculum, Teaching, and Learning at the Ontario Institute for Studies in Education, University of Toronto.

JOHN P. MILLER

Whole Child Education

University of Toronto Press
Toronto Buffalo London

KH

ISBN 978-1-4426-4260-7 (cloth)
ISBN 978-1-4426-1143-6 (paper)

∞

Printed on acid-free, 100% post-consumer recycled paper with
vegetable-based inks.

Library and Archives Canada Cataloguing in Publication

Miller, John P., 1943–
Whole child education / John P. Miller.

Includes bibliographical references and index.
ISBN 978-1-4426-4260-7 (bound).   ISBN 978-1-4426-1143-6 (pbk.)

1. Holistic education.   I. Title.

LC990.M55 2010   370.11'2   C2010-903922-X

University of Toronto Press acknowledges the financial assistance of the
Canada Council for the Arts and the Ontario Arts Council.

Canada Council   **Conseil des Arts**   **ONTARIO ARTS COUNCIL**
for the Arts   **du Canada**   **CONSEIL DES ARTS DE L'ONTARIO**

University of Toronto Press acknowledges the financial support of its
publishing activities by the Government of Canada through the Canada
Book Fund.

7/5/11

To the teachers, children, and parents of the Whole Child School

Contents

Acknowledgments

I am very grateful to the University of Toronto Press for the work they have done on this book. First, my thanks to Virgil Duff, Executive Editor, for encouraging me to submit the manuscript and managing the review process. I am grateful to Anne Laughlin for managing the production process. Thanks also to Patricia Simoes, Assistant Editor; Kim Monteforte, designer; and Ani Deyirmenjian, Production Manager, for the book's wonderful cover. I also appreciated the careful work done by copy editor James Leahy.

I am also grateful to former students who submitted their vignettes as examples of whole teaching: Glynnis Bernardo, Cyndi Burnett, Renee Cohen, Kelli Nigh, Gail Phillips, and Nancy Zigrovic. Thanks also to my graduate assistants: Jennifer Motha, who has worked in the Whole Child School, and Justyna Rucinska, who helped in editing the manuscript. I am also grateful to Stephen Davies, who reviewed the chapter on WCS, and to Deborah Adelman, WCS teacher, for her contribution to that chapter.

Finally, thanks to the Ontario Institute for Studies in Education at the University of Toronto and the many colleagues there who have supported my work in holistic education for more than three decades.

WHOLE CHILD EDUCATION

CHAPTER ONE

Whole Child Education

> The development of the mind ... and the physical and spiritual faculties of the child ... constitute an indivisible whole.
>
> – Gandhi (1980)

For the past twenty-five years educational reform has focused on testing as the way to improve student achievement. No Child Left Behind (NCLB) has been the culminating legislation of this movement in the United States. In her book *Tested,* Linda Perlstein (2007) provides a dispassionate account of how one school in Maryland has coped with the demands of NCLB. Her account describes a school day that is almost entirely devoted to preparing for the Maryland School Assessment Test (MSA), which is administered in March. Here is a typical day:

8:45–10	Mock MSA
10–11:40	Identify tone in a poem. Identify the importance of advertisements. Review parts of speech.
11:40–12:20	Lunch and recess
12:30–1:50	Language Arts
1:50–2:25	Summary of a fiction text (p. 179)

Teachers complain that there is little time for subjects such as science and social studies. The arts are totally marginalized. This curriculum makes no attempt to educate the whole child. Compare this approach to Gandhi's (1980) conception of education:

> I hold that true education of the intellect can only come through a proper

exercise and training of the bodily organs, e.g., hands, feet, eyes, ears, nose, etc. In other words an intelligent use of the bodily organs in a child provides the best and quickest way of developing his intellect. But unless the development of the mind and body goes hand in hand with a corresponding awakening of the soul, the former alone would prove to be a poor lopsided affair. By spiritual training I mean education of the heart. A proper and all round development of the mind, therefore, can take place only when it proceeds *pari passu* with the education of the physical and spiritual faculties of the child. They constitute an indivisible whole. According to this theory, therefore, it would be a gross fallacy to suppose that they can be developed piecemeal or independently of one another. (p. 138)

Unfortunately, rather than following Gandhi's vision, departments and ministries of education in most countries have followed the piecemeal approach, and the result has been disastrous. Education systems have reinforced fragmentation rather than connectedness. They have become part of a world of corporate corruption, deep distrust of politicians and the political process, environmental destruction, and an empty lifestyle based on materialism and consumption. The obsession with test results rather than a sensible approach to accountability has only led to deeper and more pervasive forms of fragmentation and alienation.

Most teachers believe in the importance of accountability measures, but only 18 per cent in one survey in the U.S. stated that the tests that they are asked to administer are useful. In this environment the creative teacher is shackled. Students focus on reading skills in a pressure cooker atmosphere where they might do well on comprehension but in the end hate reading. There is a poem being circulated among teachers that stated second graders could 'comprehend a medical textbook, read aloud seamlessly, finish all their workbooks ahead of time … but hate to read' (Perlstein, 2007, p. 82). Teachers complain that they cannot really teach anymore. One teacher said to Perlstein, 'I used to teach children to read' (p. 98). Teachers are forced to follow tightly scripted reading programs like Open Court. The result in the view of sociologist Kathy Hirsh-Pasek is that schools 'are making kids more passive' (cited in Perlstein, 2007, p. 133).

Since there is not currently a major test for kindergarten students, Perlstein found that teachers at this level have the opportunity to adapt the curriculum to the children's needs. Still, consider the standards for kindergarten students in Maryland, where they will 'algebraically represent, model, analyse, or solve mathematical or real world problems involving patterns or functional relationships' and 'use scientific skills and processes to explain the composition, structure, and interactions of matter in order to support the predictability of structure and energy transformations' (cited in Perlstein, 2007, p. 146).

Whole Child Education

There are clear signs that both educators and parents want a different approach. Certainly one of the most important is the Association for Supervision and Curriculum Development (ASCD), an organization of 175,000 educators from around the world that has identified educating the whole child as its major priority. Its annual conference and three issues of its journal, *Educational Leadership*, have focused on this issue. There is also a website, www.wholechildeducation.org.

Although England has followed the same obsession with testing, there are some hopeful signs there as well. The Department of Education and Skills commissioned a study on Waldorf schools and concluded that they had much to contribute to public education – in particular, 'the holistic approach to child development, the importance attached to spiritual values and the collegial style management' (Jackson, 2007, p. 17). As a result, the government is setting up the first state-sponsored school based on Rudolf Steiner's principles. It has also approved an inner-city school in Liverpool to become a Montessori school (p. 17).

The Department of Education and Skills in England has also shown interest in the models of child care and education adopted in other countries in Western Europe (Denmark, Holland, and Germany). This model stresses that learning, child care, and upbringing are interconnected. Jackson (2007) writes: 'In this model the child is seen as a social being, connected to others and at the same time with his or her own distinctive experiences and knowledge' (p. 18).

In Japan and Korea educators have formed groups interested in holistic education. Although Steiner education is not sanctioned by the Ministry of Education in Japan, there are now five Waldorf schools and three more are being planned. This has all occurred in the last decade.

In my own city of Toronto, three alternative schools with a holistic vision started in the fall of 2009 within the Toronto District School Board. I have been connected with one of these schools, currently called The Whole Child School. The curriculum framework for this school is based partially on my book *The Holistic Curriculum* (www.wholechildschool.

ca). There were 320 applications for the 160 student spaces in this K-5 school. The school is described in more detail in the last chapter.

Finally, the country of Bhutan, whose goal is Gross National Happiness, is embarking on an effort to base its education system on holistic education principles. The government has invited a group of educators from around the world to help them initiate this process (Miller, 2010).

The Interdependence Movement

Education needs to be based on the kind of interdependence described above in Western Europe and articulated by Gandhi. In his book *Blessed Unrest*, Paul Hawken argues that the Internet has facilitated the ability of individuals and groups to work together in a manner similar to the human immune system. Hawken describes how there a millions of these groups around the globe working to create a better world. Although they work independently, they are loosely connected by shared values; the two central values are the Golden Rule and a sense of the sacred. This collective activity can be 'seen as humanity's response to toxins like political corruption, economic, disease and ecological degradation.' A reviewer of this book cites an example of how this works:

> In January of this year seven of us – me and six brand-new graduates from Middlebury College – started a website called *stepitup07.org* asking people to organize rallies on April 14 to demand from Congress ambitious cuts in carbon emissions … We just started emails to the people we knew, and they started forwarding them and on and on. Within eleven weeks we'd organized 1,400 protests in all fifty states, one of the largest days of grassroots environmental activism since Earth Day in 1970 … We were all, I suppose, antibodies of a kind, and within a few weeks of our protests all the major Democratic candidates for president had endorsed our radical goal of eighty percent cuts in carbon emissions by 2050. (McKibben, 2007, p. 89)

This type of grass-roots movement can also be seen in education, with parent groups organizing for alternatives, as seen in the Whole Child School initiative in Toronto.

Perhaps the most powerful image of the interdependence movement is the picture of the earth taken from the moon. The picture has evoked many feelings. One is simply a sense of awe and wonder that can arise from seeing the earth against the black background of space. It is the same feeling that we get when looking at the blanket of stars at night.

Another perception that can arise is how fragile and precious the earth is. The sense of fragility gives way to a desire to care for the earth. We no longer see it as something inanimate whose resources can be used indiscriminately. Aleksandr Aleksandrov, a Russian cosmonaut, wrote: 'And then it struck me that we are children of our earth. It does not matter what country you look at. We are all earth's children, and we should treat her as our mother' (cited in Kelley, 1988, p. 110).

After he came back from space, Russell Schweickart, an American astronaut, wrote: 'When you come back there's a difference in that relationship between you and that planet and you and all those other forms of life on that planet, because you've had that kind of experience' (cited in Kelley, 1988, p. 144). Looking at the picture of the moon evokes the image of what Marshall McLuhan called the 'global village,' which everyday seems to get smaller and smaller through the Internet and modern communications systems.

The image of the earth and the efforts of people and groups around the globe to connect are providing a new context for approaching education holistically.

Teaching from the Whole

The vision of human wholeness can be traced back to indigenous people, who saw themselves as part of a whole or an interconnected web. The Greeks and Romans also referred to the 'Whole.' The Roman Emperor Marcus Aurelius (1997) wrote: 'This you must always bear in mind, what is the nature of the whole, what is my nature, how this is related to that' (p. 9). Eastern thought (e.g., Taoism, Buddhism, Hinduism, and Confucianism) is also holistic in nature. As Eckhart Tolle (2005) writes: 'The whole comprises all that exists. It is the world or the cosmos. But all things in existence, from microbes to human beings to galaxies, are not really separate things or entities, but form part of a web of interconnected multidimensional processes' (pp. 275–6).

Seeing the whole, or feeling part of the whole, has been a common thread in human experience. We see ourselves in intimate relationship with everything. Many people have had this experience being in nature, listening to music, being with family or seeing a child at play.

Having this experience we begin to see our own place in the universe and the world, and thus gain a sense of purpose. Maria Montessori called this process *cosmic education*; it is a process that can engage both teachers and students. It can also help us in seeing the whole child.

Whole child education attempts to educate the whole child (body-mind-spirit) and also connect the child to the surrounding community and the world at large.

The Whole Child

In his definition of education Gandhi said that the child includes 'head, hand, and heart'; we could also say body, mind, and spirit. NCLB and the test-oriented curriculum focuses only on the mind. Even this orientation tends to be limited to some basic skills and rarely includes critical and creative thinking. Howard Gardner (1983) has given us a much broader approach to the mind and its implications for teaching and learning. His eight intelligences include many types of thinking (e.g., logical mathematical, linguistic, spatial, musical, etc.). In teaching the whole child we need to develop reading and writing skills, but not in a mechanistic manner. Ultimately our goal is have our children love to read. Emphasis on the mechanics alone, as was suggested earlier, can actually make children hate reading and writing.

As children mature, they need to be able *to think critically and creatively*. They can solve problems that they face in their lives; they can investigate and inquire. It is often observed how the young child tends to have a natural curiosity about the world. This curiosity should be nurtured throughout the child's education. Einstein wrote that 'the most beautiful emotion we can experience is the mysterious. It is the fundamental emotion that stands at the cradle of all true art and science' (cited in Isaacson, 2007, p. 387). Einstein added: 'He to whom this emotion is a stranger, who can no longer wonder and stand rapt in awe, is as good as dead, a snuffed-out candle.' We could ask, where is this sense of the mysterious and the awe and wonder in the test-oriented curriculum?

Einstein's 'religion' was his sense that there was a beauty and order in the cosmos. So the second aspect of educating the whole child is to acknowledge that each person also has something of the mysterious within. We sometimes call this the *soul, the inner life, or the creative spark*. Emerson (1982) wrote that 'Education is the drawing out the Soul' (p. 80). To me this means we simply recognize that within each child there is the creative spark. How do we nourish this in children? Although there are some techniques that are helpful and these will be discussed in this book, perhaps the most powerful force is the loving presence of the teacher. Both Gandhi and Martin Luther King stated that love is at the centre of the universe, and likewise it should be at the heart of teaching. Teachers who are present are *there* for students, and the students can feel attentiveness and care. We have often heard stories of how a caring teacher was *the* person who inspired a student and touched that spark within that changed that student's life.

Finally, we must not ignore the *body*. There is so much evidence that something is not right in our culture when it comes to the body. On one hand, we read about how many children are overweight or even obese; on the other, we can feel distress about young women who suffer from eating disorders. A recognition of the importance of the body is the final piece in educating the whole child. It can begin with activities where children work with their hands, as in Waldorf education where they do woodworking. Young children need to *move* through games, music, and sports. Yoga is being increasingly used in schools for children of all ages as way of developing a harmonious relation to their bodies. Learning to be mindful in daily life is also a simple way of reconnecting to our bodies for both students and teachers. Remembering to take a few deep breaths during the day can help us settle into our bodies. Whole child education then focuses on embodied learning, which will be discussed in more detail in the chapter on the whole curriculum

Whole Teaching

Whole child education requires whole teaching. Since we should reach the head, hands, and heart of the student, we need a broad range of teaching approaches that reach these different aspects of the child. In the next chapter I outline three basic approaches that when used together can reach the whole child. A central theme of this book is an inclusive approach to teaching that attempts to approach the child as an 'indivisible whole.' Specifically, it focuses on how teachers can use and integrate three basic approaches: transmission, transaction, transformation. Using these approaches in an integrative way is what I call whole teaching. Let us look briefly at the approaches.

Transmission Teaching

In transmission teaching the student receives and accumulates knowledge and skills. Learning in this form can occur by reading a textbook or listening to a teacher's explanation. Knowledge is seen as fixed rather

Figure 1.1 Transmission position

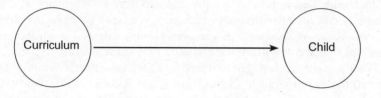

than as process and is usually broken down into smaller units so that students can master the material. Transmission teaching is common when we begin to learn a particular skill. For example, in order to drive we have to learn the basic laws and rules of driving, and thus we study the driving handbook so we can pass the written test.

When a child is learning to perform a skill, transmission teaching tends to be imitative and repetitive. The young child learns to talk by imitating the speech of his or her parents. In learning a sports skill, such as hitting a golf ball, we watch the instructor and then repeat the skill over and over.

Historically, the transmission position has a long history and has two strands. One strand is the behavioural; the second strand has focused on students studying the standard subjects taught in a traditional style (for example, lecture and recitation). In either case the relationship between the curriculum and child can be illustrated in figure 1.1.

In the behavioural strand this relationship is known as stimulus-response (S-R), while in the traditional subject curriculum, the teacher or text imparts information to the student. In both cases there is essentially a one-way flow, or transmission, of skills and knowledge and there is little or no opportunity to reflect on or analyse the information.

Regarding student evaluation, the transmission position has focused on paper-and-pencil tests and standardized tests to assess whether the student has mastered the material.

Transactional Teaching

Transactional teaching is more interactive although the interaction is mainly cognitive. The student in transaction learning is often solving a problem or pursuing some form of inquiry. Knowledge is not viewed as something that is fixed in small units but as something which can change and be manipulated. The scientific method is often used as a

Figure 1.2 Transmission position

model for transaction learning. John Dewey (1938/1969) noted that the scientific method is 'the only authentic means at our command for getting at the significance of our everyday experiences of the world in which we live' (p. 88).

As shown in figure 1.2, the transaction position can be characterized by an emphasis on dialogue between teacher and student.

However, this dialogue stresses cognitive interactions as analysis is stressed more than synthesis and thinking is emphasized over feeling. Teaching models which are based on the transaction position usually have some set of procedures for inquiry and problem solving. Sometimes these procedures are rooted in a particular discipline such as physics or history, or they are more generalized as found in various thinking skills models. The learner is generally seen as rational and capable of intelligent behaviour or as a *problem solver*.

Transformation Position

Transformational learning acknowledges the wholeness of the child. The curriculum and child are no longer seen as separate but connected. The student is not reduced to a set of learning competencies or thinking skills but is seen as a whole being. When we view the student as less than a whole person, we diminish the chance for authentic learning to occur. The teacher working from this position will use strategies such as creative problem solving, storytelling, drama, and role playing, which encourage students to make various types of connections. These connections make learning personally and socially meaningful to the student. (See figure 1.3.)

One of the key aspects of the transformation position is the recognition of the inner life of the student and how it can be nourished.

The three positions and how they can be used are discussed in more detail in the next two chapters. Whole teaching uses all three approaches

Figure 1.3 Transformation position

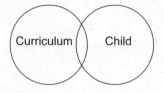

to reach the whole person. Although the transformation position explicitly deals with the whole person, the other two positions should also be used in whole child education.

The Whole Curriculum

The whole curriculum is the *connected* curriculum. It fosters relationships between subjects and various forms of thinking, and builds community. It also deepens our connection to the earth and its processes, links body and mind, and recognizes the inner life of the child. If the cosmos and the world are interconnected at every level, the curriculum should reflect this interconnectedness by focusing on relationships so that the child can see and even transform these relationships when necessary.

The fourth chapter outlines the basic features of the whole curriculum and provides a framework for developing curricula that help educate the whole child.

The Whole School

The whole school is a community; ideally, it is what Martin Luther King, Jr, called the Beloved Community. The Beloved Community is a place of both love and justice. Jing Lin (2006) has written about how we can develop this type of community in our schools. The leadership of the school is very important in this process, and the principal's role will be discussed in chapter 5, as well as staff development practices.

The Whole Teacher

A crucial element in the whole school is the whole teacher. If we are to teach the whole child, we need whole teachers. Whole teachers are teachers who care for their own bodies, minds, and spirits. They work on themselves so that they can be more whole. This may include reflective work on their teaching practices, various forms of body work, and contemplative practices such as meditation that nurture their own inner life. I have introduced contemplative practices to over 2,000 teachers over the past twenty years. Some of this work is described in chapter 6.

Whole Child School

The Whole Child School, which was launched in September 2009 in Toronto, and the framework for the school's curriculum were based in part on my book *The Holistic Curriculum* and on the ideas in this book. Chapter 7 describes the development and framework for the school and how some of the ideas of this book are being brought into practice.

Summary

Educating the whole child needs whole teaching, a whole curriculum, whole schools, and whole teachers. Although whole child education challenges administrators and teachers, it can help create schools where students enjoy being and learning. The aim of whole child education is the development of children and adolescents who can think, feel, and act and whose bodies and souls are nourished.

References

Aurelius, M. (1997). *Meditations*. Mineola, NY: Dover.

Dewey, J. (1938/1969). *Experience and education*. New York: Macmillan/Collier.

Emerson, R.W. (1982). *Emerson in his journals*. J. Porte (Ed.). Cambridge, MA: Belknap Press.

Gandhi, M. (1980). *All men are brothers: Autobiographical reflections*. Krishna Kriplanai (Ed.). New York: Continuum.

Gardner, H. (1983). *Frames of mind: The theory of multiple intelligences*. New York: Basic Books.

Hawken, P. (2007). *Blessed unrest: How the largest movement in the world came into being and why no one saw it coming*. New York: Viking.

Isaacson, W. (2007). *Einstein: His life and universe*. New York: Simon and Schuster.

Jackson, R. (2007). Hard times: Utilitarian education in England. *Encounter, 20*, 16–20.

Kelley, K.W. (Ed.) (1988). *The home planet*. Reading, MA: Addison-Wesley.

Lin, J. (2006). *Love, peace and wisdom in education: A vision for education in the 21st century*. Lanham, MD: Rowan and Littlefield Education.

McKibben, B. (2007). The interdependence revolution. *Shambhala Sun, 13*(2), 87–91.

Miller, J. (2007). *The holistic curriculum*. 2nd ed. Toronto: University of Toronto Press.

Miller, J. (2010). Educating for gross national happiness. Unpublished paper.

Perlstein, L. (2007). *Tested: One American school struggles to make the grade*. New York: Henry Holt.

Tolle, E. (2005). *A new earth: Awakening to your life's purpose*. New York: Dutton.

CHAPTER TWO

Three Approaches to Teaching: Transmission, Transaction, and Transformation

To teach the whole child we need to use a broad range of teaching strategies. If we use a limited number of approaches, we will surely not connect with the head, hands, and heart of the child.

In this chapter three basic approaches, which were briefly discussed in the last chapter, are presented in more detail. It should be noted here that I use the words *approach, orientation*, and *position* interchangeably. These terms refer to a *basic stance in teaching that is rooted in a world view.* The first part of each section briefly describes this paradigm (a more complete description of the philosophical roots of each position can be found in Miller and Seller, 1985), followed by the aims, teaching strategies, and evaluation methods. Because it is not possible to include all the teaching approaches associated with each position, I describe three teaching strategies for each position. The goal of this chapter, then, is develop a basic awareness and understanding of each of the orientations, not to identify all the strategies connected with each position.

I argue that we should use all three positions in teaching the whole child, and in the next chapter there are examples of how teachers can use them in a holistic manner. There has been a tendency for educators to engage in ideological battles; for example, traditionalists vs progressives or whole language vs phonics. We are more interested in ideas that work than ideologies that confine us. Ultimately, we seek an inclusive approach for reaching all students.

Transmission Position

In the transmission approach the function of education is to transmit facts, skills, and values to students. Specifically this orientation stresses mastery of traditional school subjects through traditional teaching methods, particularly textbook learning and the acquisition of basic skills and the inculcation of certain cultural values and mores. This last aim has led to disagreements about what should be in the curriculum, as education has become part of the current 'cultural wars.' This orientation often takes a sequential approach to learning, where skills are taught in a step-by-step sequence.

The underlying paradigm is atomism. Reality is seen in terms of separate, isolated building blocks. Information or ideas can be broken down into small, manageable units that make it easier for students to learn.

The transmission position has a long history and still has many advocates today as the best and most efficient way of teaching.

Aims

• Mastering school subjects with a focus on content. The curriculum focuses on traditional school subjects.
• Learning basic skills such as reading, writing, and basic math skills.
• Adopting basic cultural values.

Teaching/Learning Strategies

MASTERY LEARNING

Mastery learning has been advocated by several educators (Carroll, 1963; Bloom, 1981; Gallagher and Pearson, 1989; Ritchie & Thorkildsen, 1994; Davis & Sorrell, 1995) for over eighty years. The concept of mastery learning was first introduced in the 1920s by Washburne (Block, 1971), but its most famous advocate has been Bloom (1981).

Mastery learning divides subject matter into smaller units with specific objectives or outcomes. Students can work alone or in groups to reach the objectives. Criteria are set before the student can go onto the next unit. They are usually expected to be successful in mastering 80 per cent of the material.

Basing his argument that individual differences are 'man made and accidental rather than fixed in the individual,' Bloom (1981) reaches the following conclusion about learning: 'What any person in the world can learn almost all person can learn if provided with appropriate prior and current conditions of learning' (p. 136). Bloom claimed that 95 per cent of the school population can achieve mastery of the required subject matter. A crucial variable in mastery learning is time, as a mastery class usually requires 10 or 15 per cent more time to master tasks than in a conventional classroom. Bloom cited the work of Carroll (1963), who wrote that 'aptitude is the amount of time required by the learner to attain mastery of a learning task' (p. 157). In mastery learning, students receive corrective feedback to help them achieve mastery; in fact this is one of the major tasks of the teacher.

There has been extensive research on the effects of mastery learning (Guskey & Pigott, 1988; Kulik, Kulik, and Bangert-Downs (1990). One of the findings was that the learning in mastery learning tended to be enduring and not short-term. Davis and Sorrell (1995), in reviewing the research, conclude that mastery learning is 'most useful with basic skills and slow learners at both elementary and secondary levels' (p. 1).

Mastery learning can begin with diagnostic tests to see what the students know and what they need to learn to complete the unit. The material is then broken down into small, manageable units that students can master in step-by-step sequence. The diagnostic tests should be closely connected to specific instructional strategies. Bloom suggests that students tend to learn best in pairs or groups of three.

The Chicago Mastery Learning Reading Program (CMLR), originally developed for the public schools in Chicago, has also been used in California, Ohio, and Missouri. Although not specifically designed from mastery learning, current reading programs such as Open Court break down material into manageable units. Perlstein (2007) writes: 'Each reading passage was deconstructed into the basic elements (title, characters, setting); main idea ... message (quite often some version of "Never give up" or "You can't judge a book by its cover") and always, always a problem and solution' (p. 76).

PHONICS

Phonics has a long history in the teaching of reading; for example, *The New England Primer* published in 1683 used a phonics approach. For Starrett (2007):

> Phonics includes the notion of phonemic awareness, or the understanding that speech is composed of a series of individual sounds or phonemes and the ability to discern individual sounds in spoken words.
>
> Our definition of phonics includes an understanding of the alphabetical principle, or the realization that letters in words may stand for specific sounds ...

Structural analysis also comes under the umbrella of phonics ... and is a method of learning words and their meanings by noting structural changes that differentiate between words having common roots.

Finally, phonics as defined here includes the concept of syllabication, or the ability to divide longer and unknown words into syllables in order to sound them out and arrive at meaning. (p. 17)

Starrett suggests that phonics should proceed from the familiar to the less familiar and from the simple to the complex. He suggests starting with consonants, moving to vowels, and then to syllabication. The first step, he says, is learning the alphabet: 'Research over the years heavily supports the importance of learning the alphabet as a first formal step in learning to read' (p. 41). To learn the alphabet Starrett provides several games that can help the learning process, including the 'Alphabet Song,' 'Alphabet Box,' 'Alphabet Race,' 'Word Box,' 'Tongue Twisters,' 'Letter Search,' and 'Student ABC Books.'

Starrett argues for a 'balanced reading program' that includes a whole word approach; some words defy phonetic analysis (e.g., one, laugh, love) and should be taught as whole words. He also believes that whole language learning can put the reading process in a broader perspective. Starrett cites research that indicates that 'the majority of teachers embraced a balanced, eclectic approach to elementary reading instruction, and holistic principles and practices' (p. 10).

Phonics is an example of a transmission-oriented approach that can be connected to other approaches to reach the whole child.

CULTURAL LITERACY

Edward Hirsch (1988, 2002) has been one of the main proponents of cultural literacy, which focuses on learning specific information about the culture that is taken for granted in public discourse. Hirsch argues that learning to read is facilitated by the student's specific knowledge. He adopts the building block approach to knowing as information that we have already learned provides a foundation to learn more. He states that 'reading ability then depends not only on broad knowledge but also on shared knowledge' (p. xiii). This shared background knowledge is what Hirsch calls 'cultural literacy,' providing the 'foundation to further educational, economic, and social improvements' (p. xiv). Hirsch actually uses the word transmission when he writes 'Literate national language and culture are what Ernest Gellner aptly calls *school transmitted cultures'* (p. xiv). Hirsch supports Gellner's belief that the nation-state depends on school teachers who transmit the culture. If this is not done, the 'nation will decline.'

Hirsch favours a traditional subject-oriented curriculum that includes 'traditional history, myth and literature.' He argues that 'skills-oriented' programs have led to the decline in cultural literacy, which he believes is a 'mistake of monumental proportions.' Hirsch believes that a common shared cultural knowledge enables 'grandparents to communicate with grandchildren, southerners with Midwesterners, whites with blacks, Asians with Latinos, and Republicans with Democrats' (p. 5).

Hirsch outlines the knowledge that is essential for cultural literacy but does not describe teaching approaches to impart this knowledge. It is assumed that this is done through studying texts and direct instruction from the teacher.

Hirsch is clearly in favour of the traditional subject-based curriculum. This approach dates back to ancient Greece and Rome. In Greece, the seven liberal arts were taught, consisting of two divisions: the trivium (grammar, rhetoric, logic) and the quadrivium (arithmetic, geometry, astronomy, and music). Hirsch would seem to advocate a core curriculum that all students must study with a few electives.

Hirsch and his colleagues follow in the footsteps of Henry Morrison (1871–1945), who was state superintendent of public instruction in New Hampshire and later a professor at the University of Chicago. He argued for a subject-based curriculum that focused on reading, writing, and math in the elementary grades. Morrison also saw the school as transmitting cultural values, where students learn to get along with each other and accept the teacher's authority in the classroom (Gutek, 1974, p. 89).

Evaluation Methods

A variety of paper-and-pencil tests are most frequently used in the transmission approach. These can include fill-in-the-blank, multiple choice, and standardized tests.

FILL-IN-THE-BLANK TESTS

These are often teacher-developed tests to see whether students have acquired the information in a unit or lesson. Starrett's (2007) book on phonics includes a large number of these tests. For example, the test on plurals asks the student to write the plural form of a word next to the singular form (e.g., self, box, and wife).

MULTIPLE CHOICE TESTS

In these tests, also called 'selected response tests,' the student is asked to choose one answer out of four or five items. Most standardized tests contain a large number of multiple choice tests. These usually focus on knowing specific information but they can also be used to see whether students can analyse material. However, they are not helpful in synthesizing or dealing with higher thinking. These tests then tend to be limited to checking factual knowledge.

STANDARDIZED TESTS

Goodwin and Driscoll (1980, pp. 59–60) note that standardized tests have the following qualities:

• They provide a 'systematic procedure for describing behaviours, whether in terms of numbers or categories.'
• They include specified procedures for administration and scoring.
• The test items are derived from experience, either by experiment or observation, rather than theory.
• They have an established format and set of materials.
• They present the same tasks and require the same response modes from all test takers.
• They provide tables of norms to which the scores of test takers can be compared in order to ascertain their relative standing.

Standardized tests are used widely to compare schools and even countries. It is beyond the scope of this section to analyse the difficulties and perils associated with this form of test. For a critical analysis of standardized testing see the work of Kohn (1999). However, it should be noted that to assess the development of the whole child, evaluation cannot be confined to these instruments. The evaluation strategies associated with the other positions must be used.

Conclusions

Transmission teaching has a role in teaching the whole child. For example, it makes sense to break up learning into manageable pieces for some students. A short lecture can sometimes be the best way to relay information. However, this position is best used when it is combined with transactional and transformational teaching and is one of the best examples of the balanced approach to reading that includes both phonics and whole language.

Transaction Position

Transactional teaching focuses on inquiry learning, problem solving, and thinking skills. Delisle (1997) argues that 'all education involves either problem solving or preparation for problem solving' (p. 1).

Transactional teaching is based on the scientific method. John Dewey (1969/1938) wrote that the scientific method is 'the only authentic means at our command for getting at the significance of our everyday experiences of the world in which we live' (p. 88). Dewey had a broad conception of the scientific method which he applied to his problem-solving method. In the first step of Dewey's approach to problem solving, the individual confronts a problematic situation that needs to be resolved. In the second step, the person clearly defines the problem. The third step involves examining the underlying factors that contribute to the problem. In the fourth step, the individual develops hypotheses or 'if-then' statements that offer possible solutions to the problem. The consequences of various solutions are also examined. The final step involves selecting a solution and implementing it. If that solution does not work, then the person goes back and selects another solution.

Other theorists that can be linked with transactional teaching include Vygotsky, Piaget, and Bruner. In general, there is a strong cognitive focus to the transaction orientation; Piaget and Vygotosky are known for their theories of cognitive growth. For example, Vygotosky's 'zone of proximal development' is primarily cognitive in orientation.

These theorists have all been connected to constructivism, in which students create their own knowledge and meaning. Constructivist teaching is rooted in understanding how children learn and make meaning. Constructivist teaching involves moving away from a transmission approach to generate alternative possibilities and interpretations.

Aims

• To be able to solve problems. Students should be able to solve problems in variety of contexts (e.g., math, science, and everyday problems).

- To develop inquiry skills. Inquiry skills, or investigative skills, focus on gathering relevant information, analysing the information, and drawing conclusions based on evidence.
- To develop critical thinking skills. Students should be able to critically analyse generalizations and lines of argument. These skills can apply to a variety of contexts from the scientific to the political.

Teaching/Learning Strategies

PROBLEM-BASED LEARNING

Problem-based learning (PBL) is based on John Dewey's work cited above. Lambros (2002) states that Dewey 'was convinced that such an approach would create the highest level of learning among all children by tapping their interests, previous knowledge, and connection to their own world of meaning' (p. viii).

In PBL students are presented with an open-ended problem to solve and work in groups to reach a solution. In going through this process the students identify what they need to research and how to integrate information so that a solution is reached. The solution is examined against further evidence to assess its validity. Students actively participate in their own learning during this process.

PBL was adopted in 1987 at the Center for Excellence for Research, Teaching and Learning at the Wake Forest University School of Medicine. Since that time, the Center's director Dr Ann Lambros has applied the PBL principles to elementary and secondary education. In her book, *Problem-Based Learning in K-8 Classrooms: A Teacher's Guide to Implementation*, Lambros (2002) gives examples of PBL at different grade levels. She suggests that students work in groups of five to seven students. One student usually begins the process by reading the problem aloud. Next, the students make at least two lists. One is headed 'Facts' and lists all the facts that are given in the problem statement. The other list is headed 'Need to Know,' which includes information that would help them understand the problem better. The next step is to develop a list of 'Learning Issues,' which include things they need to research to help solve the problem. Following this research phase, the students list their 'Possible Solutions.' Finally, another 'Learning Issues' list is made to gather further information that can be applied to making a final choice.

An example of a problem at the grade 7 level focuses on weather forecasting. Here is the problem:

You are a weather forecaster in Morehead, North Carolina. You are currently concerned about a tropical storm off the coast of Africa. You must track and predict where it is going and when it will strike land. Once you have collected this information, you must give warnings to ships and military aircraft that could be affected by the storm. (p. 7)

The lists might contain:

Facts
We are weather forecasters.
We are in Morehead, NC.
There is a tropical storm near Africa.

Need to Know
Location of Morehead, NC
Location of the storm off the Africa Coast
Speed of the storm

Learning Issues
What is a tropical storm?
How are storms classified?
What affects the movement of storms?

The students will then conduct research on barometric pressures, ocean currents, and wind scale. They will examine the military bases that might be affected. They might also use math equations to estimate the speed of the storm and predict its movements.

Possible Solutions
This might include a couple of hypotheses about where the storm will land.

Learning Issues
Students will seek additional information that should validate one of the solutions.

Table 2.1 is a chart that students use in PBL. It focuses on the following problem: You are home alone with your babysitter and there is a severe storm warning that could cause flooding. What should you do?

Table 2.1 Completed PBL process chart, single chart

Case Name: *Weather Watch*

Fact List	Need to Know	Learning Issues
You are home alone with your babysitter.	What time is it?	How long must it storm before it floods?
	Is it dark outside?	
Your Mom and Dad are still at work.	When will parents be home?	Why do some places flood and not others?
A warning on TV says there might be a flood because of a storm.	Can babysitter drive?	How do weather forecasters know ahead of time that a storm is coming?
	Are adult neighbors home?	
		How do weather forecasters know a flood will develop from rainfall in a storm?

Possible Solutions	New Learning Issues
Call parents for advice.	Do we have an upstairs in the house?
Keep watching TV for more news.	What is high enough up if a flood starts to develop?
Go stay with a neighbor.	
	How long does it take floodwater to go away?
Go someplace higher than where we are if the storm really comes.	

Defendable Solution(s)
A safe plan showing where to go or what to do during severe weather conditions, especially when parents are not at home.
A safe plan for when parents are at home.

This or a similar form is the basic document in the PBL process. It may be structured slightly differently, or it may take two to three pages, but the categories are constant.

Reprinted with permission from *Problems – Beside learning in K-8 classrooms* by Ann Lambros.

CASE STUDY METHOD – MORAL DILEMMAS

Case studies on public issues and moral dilemmas cannot be resolved in the same manner as PBL. This is because values issues are introduced and it is not just a matter of gathering more information. All the relevant factual information should be gathered, but case studies and dilemmas encourage ethical reasoning.

Nel Noddings (2006) has recently addressed various public issues that deserve attention in our schools. Some topics include parenting, animals and nature, advertising and propaganda, gender, and the psychology of war. Many of these topics are not addressed in schools because of fear. For example, some people believe that parenting should not be discussed in public school classrooms because the public and private domains should be kept separate. Noddings believes that we need to address public issues through critical thinking. For Noddings, critical thinking includes our emotions and feelings as well as reason, and the focus is on 'self-understanding and how critical thinking may be applied to our individual lives' (p. 5).

One of the issues that Noddings addresses is gender and equality. Women still are paid less for doing the same work. One reason according to research is that women do not demand more equitable pay (Babcock and Laschever, 2003). The research also indicates that women can be good negotiators but not for themselves as they resist self-promotion. Students can discuss how women can become stronger in seeking equitable pay not just for other women but for themselves.

Another issue arises for women. Should they enter professions that are traditionally dominated by women, for example, child care, elementary education, nursing, or administration? As Noddings notes, young women can often be encouraged to go into traditionally male-dominated professions (e.g., math and science) and discouraged from going into the caring professions through statements like, 'You're too smart for that.' Noddings writes, 'To tell a bright young woman that she should study math, for example, may weaken the self-confidence she has built up through an entirely different area of study' (p. 228).

If women do work in one of the caring professions, Noddings argues that they need to help change the perception that somehow caring and the ethic of caring are less valued than other values such as cleverness and assertiveness. Noddings concludes: 'Women should probably learn how to promote themselves and protect their own interests, but society should become more appreciative of the values long associated with women. This is tough loving critical work' (p. 230).

Noddings argues for a thoughtful, reflective approach to these large issues. Originally developed by Lawrence Kohlberg (Hersh, Miller, & Fielding, 1980), the moral dilemma usually contains a conflict with two or more basic values. Discussing these dilemmas facilitates moral development as individuals are exposed to different levels of moral reasoning.

For example, in one dilemma a student sees a classmate cheating on a test. What should the student do? This dilemma raises the following issues, which can be discussed in the class. Is it more important to be loyal to a friend or to obey rules and laws? What would happen if most of us condoned cheating? Is that fair?

The teacher can ask students to take different roles in looking at the issue. For example, does it make a difference if the classmate is a close friend or someone you do not like? What should the teacher do in this situation if she or he notices the student cheating, and why? What would your parents want you to do? What would the classmate's parents want you to do?

The best dilemmas are the real ones that students face in their daily lives.

DISCIPLINED-BASED INQUIRY

Another transactional approach is the use of inquiry methods connected with a particular discipline such as math, science and history.

Biological sciences curriculum study. This curriculum is described in *BSCS Science: An Inquiry Approach* (Coulson, 2002). It encourages students to inquire into problems as a biologist would. The approach includes curriculum material for three years in secondary school. Each year begins with a two-week unit entitled Science as Inquiry and is followed by three core eight-week units that cover physical science, life science, and earth-space science. The last unit in each year is multidisciplinary and examines issues in science and society.

The students model their work on how biologists carry out scientific inquiry. The students 'learn how to conduct a scientific investigation to answer a question about the natural world and to differentiate between evidence and inference' (Bybee &Van Scotter, 2007, p. 47). In the ninth grade, students examine questions and concepts that guide scientific investigation. 'For example, what are the criteria for a scientifically testable question? (p. 47). In the tenth grade, the focus is on how to design investigations. For example, which is better in reducing germs on the hands, antibacterial soap or regular soap? In the eleventh grade, students learn how to use evidence to develop explanations and models. For example, students would look at the evidence for global warming and then consider how this evidence can help scientists improve their models of climate change.

The core unit on life science in ninth grade focuses on building blocks in nature. First, students examine the atom and then the cell. This is followed by an exploration of processes that occur around these building blocks. For example, they might measure how many calories are burned in a workout and why a muscle becomes fatigued after lifting heavy weights. In the earth-space unit, the students examine stars and how they also are building blocks in the universe.

The final unit links science and society issues and might focus on how science and technology can help in the response to natural disasters such as wildfires or volcanic eruptions.

The BSCS approach to science education began almost fifty years ago and has gone through significant developments to make it more relevant to students. However, it is still based on the idea that students can inquire into the nature of things following the model of scientific inquiry. Tests have shown this curriculum contributes to significant gains in scientific learning (Coulson, 2002).

Evaluation Methods

Assessment for transactional and transformational teaching uses a broad range of strategies to gauge the development of the whole child. The approaches discussed in the section (observation, interview, rubrics) overlap with those in the transformation position (portfolios, performance tasks, self-evaluation, and peer evaluation).

OBSERVATION

Diane Hart (1994) suggests that observation should be systematic. Here are a few guidelines:

- Observe all students.
- Observe often and regularly.

- Record observations in writing.
- Note the typical as well as the atypical observations of the routine are just as valuable as observations of the extraordinary.
- Aggregate multiple observations to enhance their reliability. One instance does not a pattern make.
- Synthesize evidence from different contexts to increase the validity of observations. (p. 16)

Next, the teacher needs to know what to look for. Here Hart suggests that developmental checklists can be used for younger children as they track behaviours related to development. She gives an example of how children playing with blocks can develop over time. This behaviour usually begins with using the blocks to make simple rows to eventually creating buildings and structures that are part of dramatic play.

INTERVIEWS

Another means of gathering data is through the interview. An interview sheet can help the teacher direct the questions and organize the evaluation data. Interviews can also be used to explore issues of self-development, such as motivation. For example, what interests does a student have in relation to a particular subject?

RUBRICS

Rubrics represent the range of behaviours with regard to a particular task that can be used by the teacher or the student to assess their performance. Below is a rubric on how a student collaborates with other students in group work.

Collaboration Rubric

4 – Thorough Understanding

Consistently and actively works toward group goals.
Is sensitive to the feelings and learning needs of all group members.
Willingly accepts and fulfils individual role within the group.
Consistently and actively contributes knowledge, opinions, and skills.
Values the knowledge, opinions, and skills of all group members and encourages their contribution.
Helps group identify necessary changes and encourages group action for change.

3 – Good Understanding
Works toward group goals without prompting.
Accepts and fulfils individual role within the group.
Contributes knowledge, opinions, and skills without prompting.
Shows sensitivity to the feelings of others.
Willingly participates in needed changes.

2 – Satisfactory Understanding
Works toward group goals with occasional prompting.
Contributes to the group with occasional prompting.
Shows sensitivity to the feelings of others.
Participates in needed changes, with occasional prompting.

1 – Needs Improvement
Works toward group goals only when prompted.
Contributes to the group only when prompted.
Needs occasional reminders to be sensitive to the feelings of others.
Participates in needed changes when prompted and encouraged. (SCORE, n.d.)

Summary

The transaction position has an important role in whole child education by helping students to think clearly and solve problems. It is much more interactive than the transmission position, as dialogue is central. However, it is primarily limited to the cognitive domain.

Transformation Position

Underlying transformative teaching is the view that everything is interconnected. Peter Senge and his colleagues (2005) write:

> Connectedness is the defining feature of the new worldview-connectedness as an organizing principle of the universe, connectedness between the 'outer world' of manifest phenomena and the 'inner world' of lived experience, and, ultimately connectedness among people and between humans and the larger world. While philosophers and spiritual teachers have long spoken about connectedness, a scientific worldview of connectedness could have sweeping influence in 'shifting the whole' given the role of science and technology in the modern world. (p. 188)

The image of the web is often used to represent this view. Fritjof Capra (1996) has described this view in his book *The Web of Life*, in which he argues that all living systems consist of weblike networks. Indigenous people have referred to the web of life while ancient Indian thought has provided the image of the Indra net, a metaphor for the interconnectedness of the universe. This net stretches throughout the universe, and at every node there is a beautiful jewel. These jewels are radiant in their beauty and are polished so that they reflect the other jewels on their surface; the process of reflection is infinite.

Aims of Transformative Teaching

The aims of transformative teaching include wisdom, compassion, and sense of purpose in one's life.

WISDOM

The ancients referred to the importance of the 'thinking heart,' where our intellectual activity is rooted in our emotional and spiritual centre. The oldest Chinese symbol for 'mind' is a drawing of the heart (Senge et al., 2005, p. 55). If we can link head and heart, then our approach can avoid empty intellectualism. In her recent biography of Abraham Lincoln, Doris Kearns Goodwin (2005) demonstrates how Lincoln made his decisions from a place of empathy that won the admiration and love of all those who knew him. Today Nelson Mandela, Vaclav Havel, and Aung San Suu Kyi are examples of leaders who work from the thinking heart.

COMPASSION/CARING

Transformative teaching also nurtures compassion. If we see ourselves as connected to others, then the compassion arises naturally since we do not see ourselves separate from other beings. Nel Noddings (1992) has written extensively on the importance of caring, which is closely related to compassion, and has suggested ways to enhance caring in the school curriculum.

SENSE OF PURPOSE

Education should help students discover a sense of purpose in their lives. Alienated youth turn to drugs and violence because they have not found deeper meaning in their lives. To give students a sense of purpose Maria Montessori developed the Cosmic Curriculum so that students would see their place in the unfolding of the universe.

Teaching/Learning Strategies

One of the best descriptions of the spirit of transformational learning was by Walt Whitman (1993) in his poem 'There Was a Child Went Forth.'

> There was a child went forth every day
> And the first object he look'd upon, that object he became,
> And that object became part of him for the day or a certain part of the day,
> Or for many years or stretching cycles of years. (p. 57)

In transformational learning, the barrier between the learner and subject disappears as the learner becomes what he or she is studying or observing. Emerson wrote that when the painter is painting a tree, the painter becomes the tree. The teaching/learning strategies attempt to facilitate this learning in which the student deeply integrates what he or she is studying.

AUTOBIOGRAPHY/JOURNALS

Having students write about themselves is an activity that can be transformative. One vehicle for doing this is having them write their personal histories. A good example of this process comes from the teaching of Jessica Siegel, whose work is described in the book *Small Victories* (Freedman, 1990). Jessica taught English at Seward Park High in Manhattan, which serves mostly the children of immigrants to the United States. In this school of 3,500 students, 92 per cent of the graduates go on to higher education.

One of the most important parts of Jessica's curriculum is to have students share their thoughts and feelings in an essay on the subject 'Who Am I?' "There are several benefits to this process. First, she saw how a powerful autobiographical essay can help a student get into college or university. For example, one student, Vinnie Mickles, had never met his biological father and his mother had been in and out of psychiatric hospitals a half-dozen times. He lived with his mother in an unheated apartment, where it was so cold that his hands froze and cracked so badly that they bled. The landlord was trying to force out the tenants so that he could raise the rent or sell the building. Because of these conditions, Vinnie could not concentrate on his work. Jessica recognized his potential and passed him. He entered the Marine Corps after graduating from Seward. After two years in the Corps, he came back to Jessica and wanted her help to get into university. Jessica had him write his autobiography: 'He delivered a devastatingly dispassionate tale of his mad mother, his absent father, his icy apartment' (p. 48). On the basis of his autobiography Vinnie was accepted at the State University of New York.

Through the autobiography Jessica gains a much more complete view of the student. She can begin to see the student as a whole person. Her instructions to the class:

> Think about your past experiences. Jot down ideas, memories, key words, whatever thoughts come to mind when I'm talking. Think of a personal object that's important to you. Why? Think about someone who has had a big effect on you. What happened? What did they say? List four or five words that describe your feelings. Pick one and illustrate with a memory from your past. List five things you're proud of. Choose one and say why it's important to you. Remember the first time you did something that stands out in your mind. Describe the incident. How did you feel about it? Have you changed in the last five years? Why? How? What made you the person you are today? (Freedman, 1990, p. 51)

Her students write about the events that have affected their lives: divorces, beatings, adultery, the near death of a parent, and even becoming a parent. One student described how becoming a father and watching the birth of his child was the most wonderful experience of his life.

After reading these autobiographies Jessica experiences a strong sense of connection to her students:

> Every year she finishes the autobiographies the same way. Her students are heroes. Her heroes, even some who fail the coursework. Could anyone else understand that? How they fill her with awe. How they, yes, inspire her. (Freedman, 1990, p. 68)

Autobiography, then, can provide a silent bond between teacher and student. Clearly, such work must be handled with sensitivity and care by the teacher. An insensitive or careless remark could hurt a student and harm the student-teacher relationship.

Other teachers use the journal as a place where students can reveal their thoughts and feelings on a more regular basis. An excellent example of the power of journals is shown in the film *Freedomwriters*, where

the students write about their lives in journals. Sharing some of the stories in the journals leads this ethnically diverse class to come together.

Yet other journals are designed to be kept in a more academic way.
These journals usually contain the student's reflections on what they
are reading and studying in class. It might include their reactions to
a novel or a science experiment. In contrast, a more contemplative
journal would contain the student's feelings and thoughts as they go
through each day. A soul journal focuses on the student's inner life. Of
course, it is important to define who is going to read the journal. There
may be portions or elements that are not open to anyone else.

ROOTS OF EMPATHY

This is a unique program developed by Mary Gordon (2005) for elementary school children. It involves bringing a mother with her baby
into a classroom over an entire school year. A Roots of Empathy (ROE)
instructor accompanies the child into the classroom as well. The students witness and identify with the growth of the baby during that
period. Mary gives several examples of how this program has reached
the most challenging students:

> Darren was the oldest child I ever saw in a Roots of Empathy class. He
> was in Grade 8 and had been held back twice. He was two years older
> than everyone else and already starting to grow a beard. I knew his story:
> his mother had been murdered in front of his eyes when he was four years
> old, and he had lived in a succession of foster homes ever since. Darren
> looked menacing because he wanted us to know he was tough: his head
> was shaved except for a ponytail at the top and he had a tattoo on the back
> of his head.
>
> The instructor of the Roots of Empathy program was explaining to the
> class about the differences in temperament that day. She invited the young
> mother who was visiting the class with Evan, her six-month-old baby, to
> share her thoughts about her baby's temperament. Joining in the discus-
> sion, the mother told the class how Evan liked to face outwards when he
> was in the Snugli and didn't want to cuddle into her, how she would have
> preferred to have a more cuddly baby. As the class ended, the mother
> asked if anyone wanted to try on the Snugli, which was green and trimmed
> with pink brocade. To everyone's surprise, Darren offered to try it, and as
> the other students scrambled to get ready for lunch, he strapped it on. Then
> he asked if he could put Evan in. The mother was a little apprehensive, but
> she handed him the baby, and he put Evan in, facing towards his chest.

That wise little baby snuggled right in and Darren took him into a quiet corner and rocked back and forth with the baby in his arms for several minutes. Finally, he came back to where the mother and the Roots of Empathy instructor were waiting and he asked: If nobody has ever loved you, do you think you could still be a good father?' (p. 6)

Mary goes on to comment that the openness and uncritical affection of a baby can be a transformative experience for children. Children respond to what Mary calls 'the wisdom of the baby.' The emotions of the baby are spontaneous and pure and have not been socialized into the masks that we tend to wear as adults. Mary writes: 'Children who have felt alienated or excluded are drawn into a circle of inclusion through the empathic contact made by the baby' (p. 7).

In the process of learning empathy, the student observes the baby's experiences and the emotions they inspire. Second, students learn to identify the emotions and 'anchor the emotions in themselves privately through discussion, reflection art and journaling' (p. 125). Finally, they talk about their feelings with other students.

Dr Kimberly Schonert-Reichal from the University of British Columbia has done research on the Roots of Empathy program and found that children who had experienced the program were more advanced in emotional and social understanding than students who had not experienced the program (Gordon, p. 246).

SERVICE LEARNING

Service Learning involves students in community activity that is also linked to academic work in the school. I would like to cite a couple of examples of service learning from two of my friends and colleagues John Donnelly and Lourdes Arguelles.

Engaged service. Engaged service is the term that John Donnelly (2002) uses to describe his work with at-risk adolescents. His students usually work with and care for physically and mentally challenged youth. The goal of this work is to develop compassion in students or the ability to see that another person's suffering is not separate from ourselves. Engaged service, then, is a process of attempting to heal this suffering in others and ourselves. John likes to use outdoor field trips to engage his students. Yet these are not just trips to see and observe nature; they also involve students helping one another. John describes one of activities that his students engaged in:

On one occasion during a field trip, ten of my students helped one student who was confined to a wheelchair gain mobility around a mountain camp that had not been adapted for children with specific physical needs. They assisted him off the bus, folded his wheelchair, set out his silverware at the table, and by splitting into three different teams, helped him hike on trails that were inaccessible to children with special needs. They finished a full day of these activities by helping him get ready and go to bed … I doubt if any more love or concern could be shown by a group of students. (p. 310)

Many of the students in this program come from extremely challenging backgrounds. One of his students was shot on the streets of Los Angeles. Yet John with his love and commitment has been able to bring hope to many of his students. He remains hopeful that we can offer an education that is truly life affirming. He writes: 'Look to the children and they will show us the way. Ask them what they need, do not explain to them what they want. Ask them how they can help do not tell them what is required. Make the subject of the day a life that can be enhanced' (p. 314).

Community-based work. Lourdes Arguelles (2002) taught at Claremont Graduate School in California. Her students ranged in age from the mid-twenties to mid-fifties. As part of the curriculum, she had them go into 'grassroots communities' which were often marginalized, either economically or socially. First, she had her students just be with people in these communities in informal situations such as 'sharing meals and casual conversation, and doing manual labor.' Second, she encouraged 'slow, non-deliberate, non-formal and sporadic ways of knowing,' which she called 'slow mind.' For some students, the shift to slow mind was a challenge:

When I first met my teacher I was not as ready for sustained and formal interaction with her as I am now. My mind was too accelerated. The time I have taken just talking and being with people at a low-income housing project sort of settled me in, and I formed a bond with the other students and with the teacher in addition to the bonds with the people in the community. I also began to realize how some of the things that I do in my classroom and in my life can impact negatively on the lives of these people. That has made a real difference in my life and in my teaching. (cited in Arguelles, 2002, p. 295)

Lourdes offered a course that challenged her students in many different ways. Through these challenges they find ways to connect more deeply with themselves and others.

Evaluation Methods

Assessment of transformational teaching and learning tends to be qualitative in nature and includes self-evaluation, peer evaluation, portfolios, and performance tasks.

SELF-EVALUATION

Self-evaluation is an important life skill, as the student learns to evaluate his or her own work fairly and candidly. After a unit is completed, students can ask themselves some of these questions:

- What was the most important thing I learned in this unit?
- Did this unit have any impact on my attitudes or values towards the topic we studied?
- What more would I like to learn concerning this topic?
- Where do I need to improve with regard to this unit?
- What was the biggest challenge I faced in studying this unit?
- What would be my overall assessment regarding my performance on this unit?

Group work can also be self-evaluated. In my courses, I ask students to self-evaluate their group presentations. They evaluate themselves according to some of the following criteria: teamwork, creativity, student response to their presentation, and the overall flow of the presentation.

PEER EVALUATION

Two widely used forms of peer evaluation are peer editing and performance in group settings. In peer editing, two students pair up and provide feedback on each other's writing with regard to spelling, grammar, and composition. In cooperative learning settings, students can provide feedback on how each member is participating in the group process. Peer evaluation is also used to assess student group presentations

PORTFOLIOS

Portfolios provide an opportunity to assess a student's work over a long period of time. They also let teachers and students become partners in the assessment process as they can decide together what goes in the portfolio. Students can also develop the habit of self-assessment through portfolios as they need to decide what to include and why they are including it in their portfolio. The possibilities of what could be included in portfolios are almost endless:

- anecdotal records
- photos
- writing (both finished and rough drafts)
- audio tapes
- artwork
- diagrams and charts
- group reports
- reflections

What ends up in the portfolio will be defined by its purpose and audience. If it is for an employer or college admission, then usually it contains only the student's best work. If it is to assess student growth over a semester, then the porfolio will include work that shows growth and development. Reflections by students on their work allow for student self-assessment. Hart (1994) gives an example of one student reflecting on the poetry he has written and included in his portfolio:

> My poems were very basic in the beginning; they were all rhymed haiku because that was all I knew about. Then I experimented with going with the feelings or ideas … don't kill yourself going over the rhymes, go with what you feel. I did that for two months. Then I started compacting them, shortening them to make deeper meaning. I could see that it would make more of a point if I washed out the the's and and's and if's. Now I am working on something different … I am not trying to write how I feel only, but metaphors. (p. 26)

PERFORMANCE TASKS

In these tasks students demonstrate their learnings, particularly knowledge and skills that are more complex. In one district they use performance assessment for evaluating writing over a three-day period. The topic is the danger of extreme cold. On the first day students begin with writing their own experiences of exposure to cold weather. Students then read a story by Jack London where the protagonist dies from extreme cold. On the second day, they write a letter to the protagonist

Table 2.2 The three positions: Aims, teaching/learning strategies, evaluation methods

	Transmission orientation	Transaction orientation	Transformation orientation
Aims	Mastery of school subjects Mastery of basic skills Adopting basic cultural values	Problem solving Inquiry skills Critical thinking skills	Wisdom Compassion Sense of purpose
Teaching strategies	Mastery learning Phonics Cultural literacy	Problem-based learning Case study method – moral dilemmas Disciplined-based inquiry	Autobiography Roots of empathy Service learning
Evaluation methods	Fill-in-the-blank tests Multiple choice tests Standardized tests	Observation Interviews Rubrics	Self-evaluation Peer-evaluation Portfolios Performance tasks

giving advice on how he might have saved himself. Students then read an excerpt from a book on hypothermia. On the third day, the students are asked to integrate information from their reading to 'write 1) a letter advising a group of friends how to prepare for and safely survive a weekend winter adventure; 2) a poem, story, or short play that captures the writer's feelings about such extreme states as intense cold, heat, hunger or fatigue; or 3) a speech designed to convince people not to travel to the Yukon' (p. 51). The final pieces of writing are evaluated in terms of their effectiveness as persuasive or informative writing.

Some schools use summative performance tasks for graduation. At Walden III High School in Wisconsin, seniors are asked to demonstrate mastery in fifteen areas of knowledge and skill by assembling a portfolio, completing a major research paper, and making a number of oral presentations. The portfolio includes a written autobiography, a reflection on work, an essay on ethics, and a written summary of coursework.

Summary

I believe that we need to use all three approaches to teach the whole child. The transmission position can help students learn basic skills such as phonics; the transaction position, with its emphasis on cognition, facilitates thinking and problem solving; and the transformation position develops self-awareness, empathy, and social responsibility (see table 2.2). The next chapter outlines a process of integrating the three positions and provides several examples of how teachers practise whole teaching.

References

Arguelles, L. (2002). How we live, learn and die: How a teacher and some of her students meditated and walked on an engaged Buddhist path. In J.P. Miller & Y. Nakagawa (Eds.), *Nurturing our wholeness: Perspectives on spirituality in education* (pp. 285–303). Brandon, VT: Foundation for Educational Renewal.

Babcock, L., & Laschever, S. (2003). *Women don't ask: Negotiation and the gender divide.* Princeton, NJ: Princeton University Press.

Block, J. (1971). *Mastery learning. Theory and practice.* New York; Holt Rinehart and Winston.

Bloom, B. (1981). *Mastery learning.* New York: Holt, Rinehart and Winston.

Bybee, R.W., & Van Scotter, P. (2007). Reinventing the science curriculum. *Educational Leadership, 64*(4), 43–7.

Capra, F. (1996). *The web of life: A new scientific understanding of living systems.* New York: Anchor.

Carroll, J. (1963). A model for school learning. *Teachers College Record, 64,* 723–33.

Coulson, D. (2002). *BSCS science: An inquiry approach* (Field test II curriculum evaluation report). Annapolis, MD: PS International.

Davis, D., & Sorrell, J. (1995, December). *Mastery learning in public schools.* Paper prepared for PSY 70: Conditions of Learning. Valdosta, GA: Valdosta State University. http://chiron.valdosta.edu/whuitt/files/mastlear.html

Delisle, R. (1997). *How to use problem-based learning in the classroom.* Alexandria, CA: Association for Supervision and Curriculum Development.

Dewey, J. (1969/1938). *Experiences of education.* New York: MacMillan/Free Press.

Donnelly, J. (2002). Educating for a deeper sense of self. In J.P. Miller and Y. Nakagawa (Eds.), *Nurturing our wholeness: Perspectives on spirituality in education* (pp. 304–17). Brandon, VT: Foundation for Educational Renewal.

Freedman, S. (1990). *Small victories: The real world of a teacher, her students and their high school.* New York: Harper and Row.

Gallagher, M., & Pearson, P. (1989) *Discussion, comprehension, and knowledge acquisition in content area classrooms* (Report no. 480). Champaign: University of Illinois.

Goodwin, D.K. (2005). *Team of rivals: The political genius of Abraham Lincoln.* New York: Simon and Schuster.

Goodwin, W.L., & Driscoll, L.A. (1980). *Handbook for measurement and evaluation in early childhood education.* San Francisco: Jossey-Bass.

Gordon, M. (2005). *Roots of empathy: Changing the world child by child.* Toronto: Thomas Allen.

Guskey, T., & Pigott, T. (1988). Research on group-based mastery learning programs: A meta-analysis. *Journal of Educational Research, 81*(4), 197–216.

Gutek, G.L. (1974). *Philosophical alternatives in education.* Columbus, OH: Charles Merrill.

Hart, D. (1994). *Authentic assessment: A handbook for educators.* New York: Addison Wesley.

Hersh, R.H., Miller, J.P., & Fielding, G.D. (1980). *Models of moral education: An appraisal.* New York: Longman.

Hirsch, E.D., Kett, J.F., & Trefil, J. (1988, 2002). *The dictionary of cultural literacy: What every American needs to know.* Boston: Houghton Mifflin.

Kohn, A. (1999). *The schools our children deserve. Moving beyond traditional classrooms and 'tough standards.'* Boston: Houghton Mifflin.

Kulik, C., Kulik, J., & Bangert-Downs, R. (1990). Effectiveness of mastery learning programs: A meta-analysis. *Review of Educational Research, 60*(2), 265–306.

Lambros, A. (2002). *Problem-based learning in K-8 classrooms: A teacher's guide to implementation.* Thousand Oaks, CA: Corwin.

Miller, J., & Seller, W. (1985). *Curriculum: Perspectives and practice.* New York: Longman.

Noddings, N. (1992). *The challenge to care in schools: An alternative approach to education.* New York: Teachers College Press.

Noddings, N. (2006). *Critical lessons: What our schools should teach.* New York: Cambridge University Press.

Perlstein, L. (2007). *Tested: One American school struggles to make the grade.* New York: Henry Holt.

Ritchie, D., & Thorkildsen, R. (1994). Effects of accountability on students' achievement in mastery learning. *Journal of Educational Research, 88*(2), 86–90.

SCORE. (n.d.). Schools of California Online Resources for Education. www.sdcoe.k12.ca.us/score/actbank/collaborub.htm.

Senge, P., Sharmer, C., Jaworski, J., & Flowers, B. (2005). *Presence: An exploration of profound change in people, organizations, and society.* New York: Doubleday.

Starrett, E.V. (2007). *Teaching phonics for balanced reading.* Thousand Oaks, CA: Corwin.

Whitman, W. (1993). *From this soil.* New York: The Nature Company.

CHAPTER THREE

Whole Teaching

How can we use the three teaching positions to teach the whole child? Since each approach reaches a different part of the child, they need to be used together in a way that nurtures wholeness. Ideally, they should be used to create a flow or rhythm in the classroom. It becomes problematic if we get stuck in one approach, as the energy can dissipate with just one method.

In this chapter I discuss the steps the teacher can use to bring the three approaches together in a holistic and rhythmic manner. Also included are descriptions of how six teachers working in different contexts have used the three approaches in their classrooms. I also include examples from Waldorf and Montessori education.

Beginning Whole Teaching

Step 1

The first step is to identify factors that can influence the selection of three positions and how they might relate to one another. Clearly one or two positions may be favoured over another because of a variety of factors. These factors include:

SUBJECT

Some subjects such as science lend themselves to transactional teaching strategies, while the lessons in the arts (e.g., drama) may be more transformational in orientation. However, other approaches can be employed to enhance and add rhythm to the learning experience.

PROVINCIAL/LOCAL CURRICULUM GUIDELINES

We can use the positions to identify the approaches advocated by policymakers. The teacher then can relate various teaching strategies to these guidelines. Guidelines today tend to focus on outcomes rather than learning strategies so that, in general, teachers have the freedom to choose the teaching approaches.

INCLINATIONS OF THE TEACHER

Teachers are often most comfortable with one approach and they should use this as their base. They can expand their approach by adding strategies from the other position. For example, if a teacher is transmission-oriented he or she can gradually include some transaction and transformational strategies.

THE STUDENT

Students vary in their learning styles. Some prefer a lot of structure and direction while others prefer more freedom and opportunities to work things out on their own. The former student, then, would probably prefer more transmission-style learning experiences while the latter student would be more comfortable with transaction and transformation approaches. David Hunt (1971) provides a framework, which he calls the conceptual level, for ascertaining the amount of structure that the student is comfortable with.

Step 2

Next, the teacher can imagine, through diagrams and metaphors, how the three positions can be connected. For example, some see the relationship in a developmental manner working from transmission to transformation (see figure 3.1).

Individuals who favour this approach see transmission teaching, with its emphasis on basic skills, providing the foundation to move onto the other two positions.

Another model employs concentric circles (see figure 3.2). Here, the size of the circles represents inclusiveness: the transformation orientation includes the other two positions in all the teaching that is done. Unlike the previous developmental model, transformation techniques could be used along with transmission methods to learn basic skills.

A third model represents the three teaching orientations in a nested

Figure 3.1 Developmental model

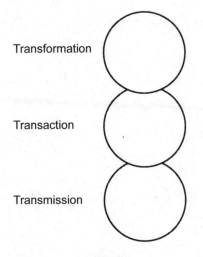

Transformation

Transaction

Transmission

Figure 3.2 Inclusive model

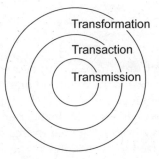

Transformation

Transaction

Transmission

design (see figure 3.3). The three positions can be used together where they intersect or separately where they do not.

In my classes I have asked students to diagram their own conception of how they see the positions relating to one another. The size of the circles can be varied to represent how much of each position is being employed. The lines can be dotted to show that positions are more fluid and can easily flow into one another. Some students use objects from nature, such as a tree, to describe the relationship in a more metaphorical manner. Like the developmental model, the roots (transmission)

Figure 3.3 Nested model

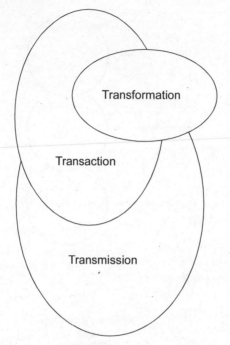

provide the base, the trunk (transaction) carries the nutrients and allows for connection between the roots and branches. The branches and leaves, which are changing, are seen as transformational. It is helpful to *play* with different conceptions to develop an overview of how you see the three positions working together to create a holistic approach to teaching. I have italicized the word play because our approach should be one of playfully creating various alternative visions through various media. I have also had students present three-dimensional models to represent their conceptions. One student created a mobile using one arrow for transmission, two interactive arrows for transaction with a moebius strip (a circle whose edge gradually twists so that both sides face in and out) surrounding the two sets of arrows (transformation).

Step 3

In this step, the teacher identifies a few strategies from each of the positions that she or he feels comfortable with. This might include a short lecture (transmission), a problem-solving activity (transaction), and a visualization exercise (transformation). For example, the students could develop a plan for building a community. They could begin by reading or hearing a lecture on urban/community planning (transmission). The students could then visualize alternative scenarios or communities (transformation). Finally, they could then work through a problem-solving process to create the plan (transaction). In selecting the strategies, teachers need to focus on the following factors:

- *Aims or outcomes*: The chosen strategies should meet the overall aim of the lesson/unit.
- *Flow*: The strategies should as much as possible create flow in the classroom rather than abrupt transitions which do not make sense to the learner. In short, the movement through the various positions and strategies should seem natural and not forced.
- *Time frame*: Sometimes there can be a tendency to plan too many activities so that students feel rushed. Make sure there is plenty of time for each activity.

Whole Teaching: Examples

The rest of the chapter provides examples of whole teaching, beginning with Waldorf Education, developed by Rudolf Steiner, and Montessori Education. Both of these approaches have a vision of the whole child that includes body, mind, and spirit. These are followed by examples from five teachers working in four different contexts: elementary, secondary, post-secondary, and teacher education.

Waldorf Education/Main Lesson

In the Waldorf school, the morning's instruction begins with the main lesson. The main lesson runs from approximately 9:00 to 11:00 a.m. In Waldorf education, the same teacher stays with the children from grades 1 to 8, and one of their main responsibilities each day is the main lesson.

The main lesson brings together English, mathematics, geography, history, and science. The main vehicle for integration is the artistic sense of the teacher. The lesson can often start with singing or a speech chorus of poems that the students are learning. Steiner recognized that young children love ritual, and it is built into many aspects of the program. The singing might be followed by teacher presentation on the main theme (*transmission*).

The arts are central to each main lesson, as it is the artistic sense that integrates the main lesson. Each student has an unlined notebook on which they draw in colour what they are learning. According to Richards (1980):

> Each Main Lesson will call upon the child's powers of listening, of body movement, of thinking, and of feeling. Artistic activity is particularly related to the will: it is an experience of doing, of making. Artwork also invites the child's feeling for expressiveness and encourages a kind of intuitive thinking about how to get things done. In the early grades, some teachers allow the children to copy what has been drawn on the board so that they may learn to draw in ways they would not otherwise know. Other times the children draw freely. Variety exists, according to teacher and grade. (p. 25)

This *transformational* approach uses wax crayons and coloured pencils as well as water colours. The student is encouraged to feel the colour as he or she draws so that the artistic experience is not abstract. In the early grades the colouring can follow the telling of a story so that language is connected to art. The student may mix primary colours such as yellow and blue to make green. Again, a story is often told before the mixing of the colours, so the experience is connected to the child's imagination. Black and white are not usually mixed at the lower grades because they are more abstract and not as dynamic for the younger child. Similarly, the children do not draw outline shapes but fill in shapes with colour. Shapes tend to come from the colour rather than from hard boundaries. Art is also connected to math as painting, modelling, designing, and string constructions are used (Richards, 1980). This aspect of the lesson is *transactional* as modelling and designing are used to help in solving math problems.

Montessori: Cosmic Education

Maria Montessori used the term *cosmic education* to refer to one element in her program for elementary-age children, which again underlines the spiritual nature of her vision. Her son, Mario Montessori (1992), describes cosmic education in this way: 'Cosmic education seeks to offer the young, at the appropriate sensitive period, the stimulation and help they need to develop their minds, their vision, and their creative power, whatever the level or range of their personal contributions may be' (p. 101). He writes that the child needs to have a 'prior interest in the whole' so he or she can make sense of individual facts. This can be done in part by introducing students to ecological principles that focus on the interdependence of living and non-living things. Mario Montessori gives the example of students studying the life cycle of salmon and its relationship with the environment.

Aline Wolf (2004) has this to say about Maria Montessori's vision of cosmic education:

> Essentially Montessori's cosmic education gives the child first an all-encompassing sense of the universe with its billions of galaxies. Then it focuses on our galaxy, the Milky Way, our solar system, planet Earth and its geological history, the first specimens of life, all species of plants and animals and finally human beings. Inherent in the whole study is the interconnectedness of all creation, the oneness of things. (p. 6)

Cosmic education helps the children place themselves within the total framework of the universe. The image of the universe presented is one of order and purpose. Since human beings are part of the universe, it gives students a common reference point beyond the boundaries created by nations and religions.

Wolf also points out that cosmic education can help children develop a sense of reverence for life and care for the earth. Seeing the miracle of life on earth within the vastness of the universe can help students appreciate more deeply life and the earth itself. Cosmic education can also give students a deep sense of gratitude as well:

> As examples, when we see a beautiful valley nestled in the mountains, we can reflect on the fact that it was formed by water that labored thousands of years to wear down the mountainous terrain, when we enter a car or train, we can look back and feel grateful to the first human being who constructed a wheel. Awareness of the long-term cosmic pattern, of which we are only an infinitesimal part, calls us to a deep humility and reverence for all the labors of nature and the work of human beings that preceded us. (p. 16)

Wolf suggests that cosmic education can give children a sense of meaning and purpose in their lives. Maria Montessori felt that within the person lay a *spiritual embryo* which needs to be nourished so that students can eventually find their own purpose on earth. In terms of teaching strategies, cosmic education can begin with the teacher reading several creation stories from different traditions – for example, 'Native American, African, Chinese, Inuit, Old Testament' (p. 91) (*transmission*). John Fowler has developed a Time Line of Light which helps children see the evolution of the earth and the cosmos. Before showing the Time Line he asks the students to close their eyes and then reads them an imaginative story on the beginnings of the universe. He then asks them to draw or paint what they saw in their visualization (*transformation*). Montessori also encouraged students to observe nature to develop a sense of awe and reverence for the natural world. She suggested that children observe a bird laying and taking care of its eggs. Children could record the number of days between the day the eggs were laid and when they were hatched (*transaction*).

Teacher Vignettes

The section includes examples of how five different classroom teachers use the three teaching positions.

Elementary Classroom: Glynnis Bernardo

I teach in a Catholic elementary school and part of our Religion program has an aspect of social justice. One day, we had reached a lesson on the disparity between the rich and the poor in the world. I was new to teaching grade 3 and I did not expect much to happen in my lesson. I ignorantly assumed that eight- and nine-year-old children would not find any connection to people who had less than them. I was wrong.

In the Religion teacher's manual, one of the suggested lessons was to disproportionately hand out 'tickets' to several students. At first, students watched and wondered what was happening. Then the questions began: 'What about me?' 'You forgot to give me one!' 'How come he got more than me?' After a few moments, I said to my students, 'I'm sure you're wondering what those red tickets are for … well, anyone who has a ticket is allowed to use it to "buy" a break. If you have a ticket, you can give it to me and choose to do something – anything – like playing on the computer, watching a movie, or even going out to play soccer.'

'But what if we didn't get a ticket?' one student asked.

'Well, I'm really sorry. You'll have to stay with me and do work.'

Automatically, the students who did not have any tickets cried out in protest, proclaiming that it wasn't fair, while those that had one or more tickets smiled and gloated.

We talked about each group's feelings, and I spoke to them about how in life, sometimes things are not fair. Sometimes people are lucky to have a lot of things while some have fewer or nothing at all.

I recollected the tickets for my next example. I gave six students four tickets each and I separated them from the rest of the class, who had none. One student noticed that if the six students shared, there would be just enough so that everyone could have one ticket. She concluded that it would be fair and no one would be left out.

We discussed this realization, and I told them about the division between the northern and southern hemispheres. I told them that there were fewer people in the northern hemisphere just like our six people, and more people in the southern hemisphere just like our students who had no tickets at all. I was careful to point out that this was just a demonstration – there are many rich people in the southern hemisphere and poor people in the northern hemisphere – I was using the tickets to make a point. 'Did you know that there is enough food in the world to feed everyone if we all shared?'

This question led to a very interesting discussion. The students discussed reasons why people do not share food through a think-pair-share. Their reasons were: people were greedy, people didn't want help, or people should work for it.

One student raised her hand, 'Look, I want to give things to homeless people. But let's say I give them money and they use it to buy cigarettes … cigarettes kill people so why should I give them money if they're going to spend it on something that's not good for them?'

It was at this exact moment that I felt magic happen in my room. It was a very good question.

A boy raised his hand and said, 'When I grow up and get a job and I start making money, I'll want to give poor people money. But if I'm working hard and the homeless person could work but doesn't want to, why should I give money if they're not looking for a job?'

What great questions from my students!

My analysis:
The lesson in my classroom demonstrates all three modes of teaching. *Transmission* was used in my lesson when I gave information and facts about the disparity between the rich and the poor. I shared my knowledge with my students under the assumption that they did not know much about

the subject area. My students' discussion and experience with the disproportionately distributed tickets demonstrates *transaction* because they were interacting with each other and developing their own ideas about poverty. The *transformational* moment was when the young girl began to question if her good intentions to give money could result in killing another person. It was at this moment that my students' views on poverty changed – they discovered that there was no simple way to resolve it.

Secondary Example (French): Nancy Zigrovic

As a classroom teacher in a public secondary school in the province of Ontario, performing the daily balancing act between ministry, school, and community expectations is no small task. I have found that the incorporation of the three positions of transmission, transaction, and transformation into my daily classroom practice has provided me with a framework for making meaningful connections with students. I will offer a recent unit of study that I shared with a grade 12 French Immersion class as an example.

Because the thirty grade 12 students sitting before me during first period had reached the final semester of their high school experience, I proposed to them that we use the central theme of 'Leaving a Legacy' throughout the semester. We began each morning with a short five-minute meditation (*transformation*). The students reported that they began the day feeling more relaxed and focused, and have told me since that meditation is a skill they continue to use in their busy lives. Next, we moved into shared reading of important French literary works, including *L'Étranger* by Albert Camus. As we read together, I provided lectures on the philosophy of existentialism and/or lessons on important grammatical structures and vocabulary taken from the text *(transmission)*. From time to time, small tests and quizzes were used to evaluate student learning.

To continue building on our central theme, we often followed our shared reading with open discussion on topics such as Camus's legacy, positive and negative legacies left by historical figures, and legacies that are being left in society today (*transaction*). Student learning was assessed through oral response, and, from time to time, a written response based on a particular discussion was evaluated. In addition, the students completed research assignments on related topics. They shared their findings with one another during short oral presentations (*transaction*) and by the end of the semester had written an impressive research essay.

To provide space for the students to create their own meaning around the idea of legacy (*transformation*), each student completed a 'Legacy Project' throughout the semester. I encouraged the students to use this time to do something that they had always wanted to do that would chronicle the legacy that they were creating in their own lives. For example, one student was unhappy with her relationship with her grandfather. For her legacy project, she volunteered at his long-term care facility and now shares a much closer relationship with him. Another student spent time learning about Catholic doctrine in an effort to understand his family's strong French Canadian ties with the Church. Yet another student had always wanted to finish writing a book that she had started in her grade 11 year. She finished it during the semester. Each day, we devoted the final part of class to working on these projects. I met with students individually to discuss progress and setbacks. They worked together to problem solve. During the final two weeks of classes, the students presented their culminating Legacy Projects to me and to one another in five small groups of six students. Teacher and peer evaluation of these projects was completed using an evaluation rubric that the students and I created together. Students who had known one another for years commented time and again on how much they had learned about one another. And most importantly, each student had learned something new about himself or herself.

Secondary: Renee Cohen

In my work as an educator, I use storytelling, visualization, and sharing circles in order to foster a sense of community, create a room full of reflective artists, and provide a reference point for learning and growth. In the following lesson ideas, I use all three learning approaches including transmission, transaction, and transformation in the hopes of developing a sound arts-based holistic learning environment for my students. While some students stop at the transmission stage, others weave in and out of all three areas of learning, thus creating transformational and life-changing moments.

At least once a week, I read my high school drama classes a children's book in order to activate their imaginations, allow them to connect the story to their own life, and to draw parallels to classroom learning. The beautiful pictures and wonderful messages enable the students to dig into their childhood imaginations and light the fire needed for a positive learning environment. Simply reading the books to the students indicates the *transmission* approach to learning or the stimulus-response methodology.

The following activities are *transactional*, as social reflection is a necessary part of this experience. Students need cognitive interaction with the ideas in the stories to make the connections to their own lives and their own educational journeys. To quote Donna Norton, 'Literature entices, motivates, and instructs. It opens doors to discovery and provides endless hours of adventure and enjoyment.' (Norton & Norton, 2002, p. 4). The topics of these children's books include: the imagination, stage fright, creativity, and perspective among others. The relationship between these stories and the course are very strong, thus helping my students realize that they are not alone in their fears and that their feelings are perfectly normal.

In addition, every Friday or the last class of the week, the students take part in a sharing circle. While sitting in a circle on the floor, students are given about ten to fifteen minutes to share a 'highlight' or a 'lowlight' from their week. Students may of course choose to pass; however, most students choose to share at least one thing with the group. This is a real highlight from our week. Students develop a comfort level with a group and feel safe sharing personal stories and anecdotes with the class. They work through their personal challenges with their peers and make decisions about real social problems. In this activity, we see the transaction approach to learning. Students use problem-solving and thinking skills to openly work through difficult adolescent situations. Here the students are not simply taking in the information being taught, but rather they are actively learning in a student-centred activity. I find that this sharing circle gives students the safe space for opening their minds, hearts, and souls to the larger group.

Finally, the last practice that I will address will be the guided imagery exercises, which are *transformational*. From my experience, imagery has the potential to bring about a transformative learning experience for students by 'promoting personal growth and social change.' Each week, I plan to do one visualization or relaxation exercise with the students. I also allow students to request them if they feel they need them on a particular day. I try to lead the students through these exercises on the days of their major presentations and performances. I find that asking students to close their eyes, breathe, and use their imaginations gives them a tremendous sense of calm and energy. I also use the visualization as introductions to difficult drama or acting material in order to provide students with a visual reference for their work. This teaching methodology allows the student and the text to be connected in a real and practical way. It incorporates the whole person, 'the head, the heart, and the hands,' thus enabling the students to engage in meaningful and authentic transformative learning.

Recently, I reflected back on my teaching metaphor, which I created quite early on in my professional career. I realized that it is one thing to have the metaphor on paper and hope that it comes true and another thing to actually become the metaphor. In my readings, I came across a guided imagery entitled 'The Butterfly.' I said to myself, 'wouldn't it be perfect if I could take my students on a mental journey in order to give them the framework to actually become those beautiful butterflies that I dreamed about in my teaching mission statement?' One day in class, I led the students on the following image exercise. 'Imagine a caterpillar. You can watch it crawling about on the tree where it lives ... Gradually it surrounds itself with golden silken threads until it is totally hidden ... Now be inside the cocoon ... At last the cocoon breaks open, and a ray of light penetrates through a chink ... As you feel the cocoon falling away, you discover that with it you have shed the defences and supports of your safety and your past. You are now freer than you ever dreamed you could be; you are a beautiful, multicoloured butterfly' (Ferrucci, 2004, p. 121). At the end of this journey, I asked the students for feedback and reflections. One student, the shy and timid student in the class, put up his hand with a great deal of energy and said, 'It was amazing that I actually saw myself as the cocoon.' After hearing this comment and seeing the smiles on the students' faces, I realized that the visual reference really worked. Enabling students to become the object gave them the perspective they needed to move forward.

In my teachings, I always struggle with how to make the learning the most experiential it can be. I strive to make the classroom experiences practical and applicable to life itself. So often, we are taught concepts and frameworks that have little to no relevance to our day-to-day lives. While learning may not always have an immediate application, it should have some connection to our existence on this planet.

Kelli Nigh (Drama)

Teaching drama is an opportunity to actively engage the whole student. Over the past few years, it has been a particular challenge to give practical instruction on the fundamentals of breathing and the voice. So many wonderful productions suffer because either the students were inaudible or their voices were pushed, sacrificing months of preparation only to *shout*

out the character during the final culminating activity. Giving a student a microphone does not ameliorate the problem long-term. Learning to carry the voice throughout a space is fundamentally related to awareness, an awareness that evolves through knowledge, experimentation, and significant sensual experience.

There is a fair amount of controversy among experts as to the most effective approaches to vocal training. Some approaches are technical (or mechanical), explaining and exercising each area of sound production in the body, face, and mouth. Other metaphysical approaches aim to access the whole body, cultivating a connection to the voice through breathing and visualization. Both approaches exemplify a continuum between disciplining and freeing the voice. Technical skills can be presented in such a way that the skill, even though requiring repetition, is learned through exploration and play. Some students prefer to take a visualization journey that leads them throughout the body, and then to hover over the room, float over the city, through the sky, into the sun and back again, finding home in the solar plexus. The enjoyment derived from the freedom of this journey comes through the sounds the students create. Within these two schools of thought the transmission, transaction, and transformation teaching methods are possible.

Beginning voice at the start of the year, I demonstrate how the students practise breathing, prone on the floor, both hands lying gently on their stomachs. I emphasize the need to allow the body to become a channel to the breath. The stomach expands on inhaling, contracts on exhaling. Eventually we practise making sound, a slight sigh on the exhale. These mini-demonstrations rely on the *transmission* teaching method. The specific pedagogic attention at this time is on relaying what the student must do to learn the basic voice skills. A special emphasis is placed on safety and accuracy. Accompanying experiential demonstrations are diagrams that explain, for example, the function of the diaphragm, the larynx, and the hard palate.

After the basic skills have been introduced, the students work together. This learning phase follows the *transactional* method of teaching because the students expand their awareness to breathing and sound by experimenting and talking with a partner. The transactional method makes room for the students to accept the tensions that may be felt in the body, without feeling as if they have failed at a particular skill. The learning emphasis is on exploration. I initially ask questions that point to what the process feels like in the body. While one student may identify that they hold tension in the shoulders, the observing student may notice or hear tension in another area. Together the students strategize as to how they may further explore their vocal habits and potential.

Over several years, however, I discovered that despite my demonstrations, student exploration, and countless visualizations, the students were not obtaining a real mastery over vocal resonance. Some students said that they experienced fleeting moments where they could feel resonance. Commonly a slight vibration would be felt in the nose or mouth. However, the *transformation* exercises I used were designed for the individual. Tobin Hart (2001) writes that during the transformational experience we go beyond current form. When we do this, we 'ride the crest of the waves of creation, a wave that constantly collapses and rises into new forms' (p. 129).

One morning the students and I experienced resonance as a collective experience; we rode the sound waves, so to speak, of the entire class. The class agreed to do some toning, each student hummed a single note, and we all joined in, sustaining the note for a good three minutes. Intermittently the students would take breaths and continue singing the solitary note. On this particular day, a flutter was felt in the atmosphere. The students began describing the feeling of the sound, as it seemed to wave throughout the room. One student dipped her hand into the middle of the circle as if it was a pool of water and said, '*I can feel the group.*'

By voicing her experience, this student allowed us all to touch down on shore for a while, concretizing a phenomenon that we were only on the edges of understanding. Using the *transmission, transaction, and transformation* approaches to teaching and learning facilitates an attunement to the needs of the whole individual and the whole class.

Post-Secondary (Creative Problem Solving): Cyndi Burnett

I teach an undergraduate course, based on a deliberate problem solving process, called Creative Problem Solving (CPS), at the International Centre for Studies in Creativity, Buffalo State. The process focuses strongly on the cognitive aspects of problem solving and pays very little attention to affective and intuitive aspects.

Although CPS is regarded as a very effective system, I felt disconnected from it when I initially learned the process because it didn't recognize the way in which I typically solved problems. While I felt it opened the door to looking at problems from a logical perspective, I continued to feel a significant piece of the process was missing.

When I first began to teach the course, I used the design provided by my colleagues. This primarily employed the transmission and transaction approaches in my classroom. The *transmission* approach was used to: review the fifty-year history of the CPS process; compare and contrast the numerous problem-solving models in existence; provide information and guidelines on the various tools and techniques; and to supply examples of how they were applied in various settings. These tools and technique were designed to develop the cognitive abilities of flexibility, fluency, originality, and elaboration in creative and critical thinking. The application of these tools, combined with the natural flow of the course content, enabled me to easily incorporate the *transaction* position into the curriculum. Over the course of the semester, students came up with challenges and had to problem solve using the various tools that they were given. They were frequently challenged to think in different ways based on the situation at hand.

Unfortunately, after teaching the course for the first time, I recognized that many of my students had experienced the same feelings of disconnect which I had encountered previously. I felt as if I was building their ability to problem solve with their minds, but not with their hearts or spirits. Reflecting on my own experience with the process, I realized that the students – while they gained new skills with CPS – were not emotionally engaged. Having come to this realization, I began to research other problem-solving approaches in the hope that they might bridge this apparent gap. I explored a number of approaches including the labyrinth, use of metaphors, and reflection activities involving collages, and journal entries to help support the CPS process. In addition, I began to research emotional intelligence and intuition, specifically its impact on problem solving. My research made me realize that it might be possible to merge these different approaches with the core CPS model. I therefore revisited some of the basic CPS tools in an attempt to make them more holistic.

For example, in the CPS process there is a stage called 'data collecting.' Typically, I taught data collecting by having students collect all of the information around the given situation. However, I have modified data collection into a model called ASC – Affective, Spiritual, and Cognitive. Students begin by collecting all the things they can measure with their minds (the Cognitive). They write the facts and the who, what, where, why, and when around the situation. Next, they collect the emotions around the situation (Affective). How do they feel? How do others feel about this challenge? What are some implications of this challenge with regard to relationships? Then, I have students think about their inner selves (Spiritual). What does their gut tell them to do? How are they feeling connected or disconnected to this challenge? How is their culture influencing their inner values and beliefs? Finally, I have the students look at the whole picture. What do they notice? Where are the biggest challenges? What do they have the most/ least control over?

I began to weave my new-found knowledge into my CPS course the second time I taught it. In making the CPS tools more holistic, I found students connected more with each another, with me, and most importantly, with themselves and the challenges they faced. Additionally, I built in a segment using service learning, where students were taking their skills and using them to help their community. This was the *transformational* position in action, and it was very powerful. They weren't afraid to look beyond the facts, and into the feelings and intuitions they had about a difficult situation. In the final student reflection papers, I reviewed the impact of the transmission, transaction, and transformational positions I had brought to my classroom. The impact of the holistic perspective was clear: it created the type of learning that developed effective creative and critical thinkers who were connected to themselves and to the world around them.

Teacher Education: Gail Phillips

I teach pre-service students at a Faculty of Education. Ours is a 'Tribes' classroom. Jeanne Gibbs (2006), the founder and author of the process called Tribes Learning Communities, believes that student well-being and success are 'not a result of curriculum, instruction and assessment – nor of intelligence – but the result of a school focusing on the growth and whole human development of its students in all aspects of their individual uniqueness' (p. 431).

My first year at the Faculty of Education was an extraordinary one and I smiled on the last day of class as I watched my students excited and ready for the next step in their adventure. Their growth during the year had been incredible. As I looked around the room, however, I was struck by the fact that all of my students had 'their own' chair and table.

During the summer as I reflected on the year and planned for the next, one of my goals was to put processes in place so that everyone didn't have their own chair. For this reason, I began to weave the belief systems of Tribes together with a variety of instructional strategies to create a learning community. A learning community is particularly important since the pre-service year is not only a crucial one in terms of teacher development but also a stressful one. Students need to ask their instructors and colleagues the tough questions that can lead to profound learning through discussion and problem solving. This requires a safe, collaborative learning environment with multiple opportunities to teach and learn with a variety of groups in many different chairs.

During our weekly classes I use and integrate the three positions: transmission, transaction, and transformation. At the beginning of the year, I introduced the Tribes process and four agreements of Attentive Listening, Mutual Respect, Right to pass, and Appreciation/No put-downs (*transmission*). Through small group discussions and tasks the students had discussed the agreements and how to introduce and practise them in meaningful and integrated contexts (transaction). Partway through the year, I introduced the concept of a *Talking Stick*. A Talking Stick is a tool used in many First Nations' traditions at council meetings. It allows all members to present their points of view. The Talking Stick is passed from person to person and only the person holding the stick can speak. The others listen. In the circle everyone teaches and learns together. I modelled the steps to create a Talking Stick and explained how one is used (*transmission*). Students worked in grade groupings (K–2, 3–4, 5–6, 7–8) to discuss how Talking Sticks could be integrated into their planning not only to reinforce concepts in the Ontario curriculum but also to practise the Tribes agreements and specific social skills (*transaction*). The students then chose their materials (tree branch, coloured yarn, ribbon, feathers, beads) and began to create their own Talking Stick. You could feel a quiet energy as they held the tree branch in their hands, wrapped their wool around it, and added feathers, beads, and ribbon. As they created their Talking Stick, I asked the students to think about two things: a song and a place that had special meaning for them. Once they had finished making their Talking Sticks, mine was passed around the circle. It was as if time had stopped. As the students held the Talking Stick, each one shared the song and the place that they had chosen. It was quickly evident that something magical was happening. The Talking Stick became a Listening Stick as each one of us gave our full attention to everyone else in turn. We listened with our ears, eyes, and hearts. We were consciously present in the moment. There were nods, tears, smiles, and hugs as people spoke and listened from the heart. We were all transported into each other's lives. Simple questions gave voice to profound stories, deepening bonds and connections (*transformation*). We were one, yet it was not the Talking Stick alone that united us. It was the process that allowed each of us to develop a deeper sense of listening, well-being, and belonging to the group.

After all of the stories had been shared, each of us placed our Talking Stick on a black cloth on the floor to create a beautiful star shape that radiated with energy and reflected the uniqueness, the wholeness, and the power of the circle.

Conclusion

Whole teaching is more an art than a science; thus, it calls upon teachers to use their intuition in deciding what strategy to employ and when to use it. Even though I have offered steps and guidelines for whole teaching, teachers should not take a mechanical approach in using the three positions. Working from their intuition, teachers can then develop their own rhythm to reach the whole child. In this way whole teaching develops organically from within teachers and becomes a genuine and felt experience for both themselves and their students. The teachers in the examples above have worked in this manner.

References

Ferrucci, P. (2004). *What we may be.* New York: Penguin.

Gibbs, J. (2006). *Reaching all by creating tribes learning communities: A new way of learning and being together.* Santa Rosa, CA: Center Source.

Hart, Tobin. (2001). *From information to transformation: Education for the evolution of consciousness.* New York: Peter Lang.

Hunt, D. (1971). *Matching models in education.* Toronto: OISE Press.

Montessori, M. (1992). *Education for Human Development: Understanding Montessori.* Oxford, UK: Clio.

Norton, D., & Norton, S. (2002). *Through the eyes of the child: An introduction to children's literature.* Englewood Cliffs, NJ: Prentice Hall.

Richards, M.V. (1980). *Toward wholeness: Rudolf Steiner education in America.* Middletown, CT: Wesleyan University Press.

Wolf, A. (2004). Maria Montessori cosmic education as a non-sectarian framework for nurturing children's spirituality. ChildSpirit Conference, 7–10 October. Pacific Grove, CA.

CHAPTER FOUR

The Whole Curriculum

The whole curriculum is the *connected* curriculum. The whole curriculum focuses on relationships so that students can make connections. One of the fundamental realities of nature is interdependence, yet our curriculum is fragmented as we break knowledge into courses, units, lessons, and unconnected information. Whole child education focuses instead on the connected curriculum.

In this chapter we examine six types of connections. The whole curriculum does not isolate information and concepts but shows *relationships among subjects*. It supports an integrated approach to learning. The whole curriculum also connects the student to *community*. This includes the classroom community, the school, the surrounding community, and finally the global community. Within the community the whole child can grow in a caring environment. The whole curriculum also connects the student to the *earth* and its processes. This can happen through activities such as gardening or reading indigenous people's literature.

At a more individual level, the whole curriculum connects different forms of *thinking*, particularly analytic and intuitive thinking. It seeks whole-brain learning. It also seeks to connect *body and mind* so that students feel 'at home' in their bodies. The problems of obesity and eating disorders among the young indicate that many children do not feel connected to their bodies. Finally, the whole curriculum connects the person to the deepest part of their being, the *soul*. Rachael Kessler (2000) and others (Miller, 2000) have shown how this can be done in a manner that respects a person's faith.

Figure 4.1 Integrated/holistic curriculum

Multidisciplinary	Interdisciplinary	Transdisciplinary or Holistic
Separate subjects; there may be some linkages through content	Integration of two or three subjects around problems, questions, or limited themes	Integration of nearly all subjects around broad patterns or themes

◀───▶

Transmission	Transaction	Transformation

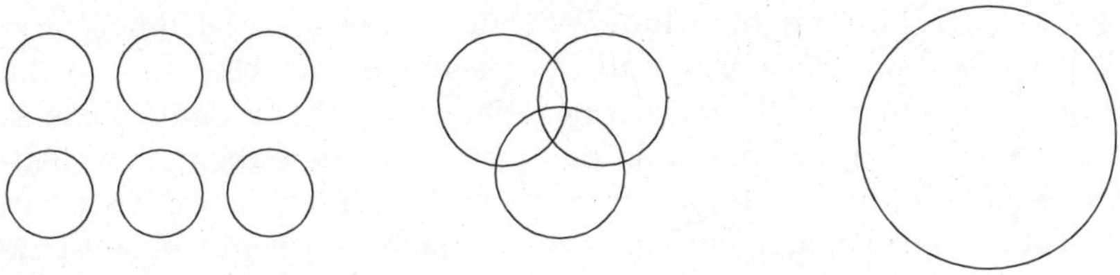

Subject Connections

Connections among subjects are also referred to as integrated curriculum. This can occur at a number of levels (figure 4.1). The first level is the *multidisciplinary*. Here the curriculum retains separate subjects, but the teacher in one subject makes a link to another. For example, the history teacher might reference the literature and art of a specific historical period and explore how the art was representative of that period. At the *interdisciplinary* level, two or three subjects are integrated around a theme or problem. For example, if the class is examining the problem of city traffic and other problems of urban planning, subjects such as economics, political science, design technology, and mathematics can be brought together and integrated. At the *transdisciplinary* level, several subjects are integrated around a broad theme. Issues such as poverty and violence lend themselves to this broadly integrative approach. At each level, connections between subjects and concepts become more numerous and complex.

James Beane's Integrated Curriculum

One of the best approaches to integrated curriculum has been developed by James Beane (1997). He believes that the curriculum should move away from fragmented approaches where knowledge is kept within the boundaries of separate subjects. For Beane, integrated curriculum focuses on issues of personal and social significance. A key feature of Beane's approach is the student input in curriculum planning. He suggests that students participate by identifying questions related to personal issues and those that are oriented towards society and culture. The former could include questions such as 'What kind of job will I have when I become an adult?' and 'Will I get married?' Society-oriented questions might include 'Why do people hate each other?' and 'Will racism ever end?' After all the questions have been put on the board or chart paper, the teacher negotiates with the students' themes, or organizing centres, based on the questions. These themes are usually broad and include topics such as 'conflict and violence,' 'living in the future,' and 'money.' Beane suggests using a concept web with the central theme in the middle and a number of sub-themes surrounding it. The students research the theme and sub-themes and then present their conclusions through some kind of activity or performance. For example, a class focusing on the environment could divide into five subgroups to create five large-scale biomes in their classroom. Another class working with the theme of living in the future could develop a vision of what their city will be like in the year 2030.

Room 56 and the Hobart Shakespeareans

Rafe Esquith teaches in an inner-city elementary school in L.A. and his work has received national recognition. One of the unique features of his program is that his students present a Shakespeare play at the end of the year. However, this project is not just about presenting a play but using the play to connect different subjects and ideas. Esquith (2007) writes: 'I have found no other project that allows me to teach the students everything I want them to learn in a single activity' (p. 208). The students learn not only the power of language, but also music, dance, and the art of storytelling. They learn to explore themes in the plays and apply the ideas to their own lives. In Esquith's words, 'They will analyse, dissect, tear down, and then build a play that will change their view of themselves and the world' (p. 208). Although the plays always receive standing ovations, for Esquith the process of working together is what leads to significant change. The actor Sir Ian McKellen has seen the Hobart Shakespeareans and has commented on how these young people know what the words mean, which he states cannot be said of all Shakespearean actors.

All the work is done after school by students who volunteer and commit to working the entire school year. This means no television or video games for that time. The students can come from other classes besides Room 56. They begin by reading a summary of the play so that they understand the story, characters, and main themes. After reading the summary of the play, they listen to a recorded performance. Esquith plays the CD and stops at different points to explain various phrases. He also shows the film of the play that they will be doing.

To familiarize students with the language, Esquith uses an exercise based on the essay 'On Quoting Shakespeare' by Bernard Levin. This can be found through a Google search, and it contains expressions from daily life that come from Shakespeare. Some of these phrases include 'vanished into thin air' or 'too much of a good thing.' He has the students say the quotes in rapid sequence.

The play itself is put on right in the classroom with bleacher seats that allow thirty-three people to see the play. Pop music that is relevant to the play's theme is used. The students sing and dance to the music that is interwoven with the text of the play. For example, John Lennon's 'Jealous Guy' was used when Leontes asks for forgiveness in *The Winter's Tale* and REM's 'Everybody Hurts' was layered over Hamlet's 'To be or not to be' soliloquy. Professional choreographers are used to teach the students two or three dance numbers for the play. Again, modern music is used for the dance that is linked with the text. The students performed a dance based on Dusty Springfield's 'Wishin and Hopin' to satirize the Katherine character.

Esquith states: 'Speaking Shakespeare's words, playing great songs, and dancing through it all is a killer combination. The kids have so much fun rehearsing, they hardly realize how much they are learning' (p. 220). PBS did a television program on Room 56, in which one student was asked to name his favourite book. When asked why he picked *The Adventures of Huckleberry Finn*, the boy said: 'Mark Twain held the mirror up to nature.' Esquith comments: 'Without blinking an eye, this student was using Hamlet to express his own beliefs and thought. I guess the poet and dramatist Ben Jonson was right: Shakespeare was not of an age, but for all time' (p. 223).

Community Connections

The Classroom

Fundamental to reaching the whole child is providing a caring community. This, of course, begins in the classroom. The teacher sets the tone for the class through his or her presence. Through both the verbal and non-verbal behaviour, teachers create community in the classroom. Nel Noddings (1992) has written extensively about caring in education, which is first manifested with the attentiveness of the teacher. If the children experience this attentiveness, they will feel comfortable in the classroom; however, teachers who are thinking about something else while the child is talking to them create a distance between themselves and the student. Children sense immediately when we are there. Non-verbal behaviour is especially important. Tone of voice and eye contact convey messages that can be more important than any words that are spoken. An encouraging smile from the teacher can also create a positive tone. In chapter 6 I will discuss the work that I have done with teachers in enhancing their presence through meditation and mindfulness. These teachers state that through these practices they are able to step back from troublesome situations. Here is the comment of one teacher who has done work with meditation and mindfulness practices:

> You can get really frustrated with these kids because they get really angry and frustrated because they can't read, and your first response is to be an authoritarian, when actually they just need to be hugged and loved. So it [the meditation] really helps me to step back and look at what really is going on.

Strategies such as cooperative learning also help create community. Students can get to know each other better when they work together in small groups. Cooperative learning can take many forms. Roger and David Johnson (1994) suggest that in cooperative learning students feel responsible for others students' learning as well as their own. For example, in a spelling lesson students could work in small groups to help each other learn the words. For the Johnsons cooperative learning includes the following elements:

1. clearly perceived positive interdependence,
2. considerable promotive (face-to-face) interaction,

3. clearly perceived individual accountability and personal responsibility to achieve the group's goals,
4. frequent use of the relevant interpersonal and small-group skills,
5. frequent and regular processing of current functioning to improve the group's future effectiveness. (p. 2)

POSITIVE INTERDEPENDENCE

Positive interdependence means that students believe that they 'sink or swim together' as opposed thinking only about themselves. This means the students not only learn the material or skills themselves but also ensure that all members of the group learn the material as well. The element of positive interdependence is related to the concept of interconnectedness, which is so fundamental to integrative teaching and holistic learning. The Johnsons suggest that this interdependence can be facilitated in different ways. One way is through positive goal interdependence, in which students focus on a common goal. Another way is through positive reward, which celebrates interdependence; for example, the group might receive bonus points if everyone meets the basic criterion on a test or assignment. A third way to foster interdependence is to encourage the group members to share resources. Finally, interdependence can be facilitated through assigning group members various roles. Glasser (1986) identifies four roles for group members:

1. Encourager of participation: in a friendly way encourages all members of the group to participate in the discussion, sharing their ideas and feelings.
2. Praiser: compliments group members who do their assigned work and contribute to the learning of the group.
3. Summarizer: restates the ideas and feelings expressed in the discussion when appropriate.
4. Checker: makes sure everyone has read and edited two compositions and that everyone understands the general principles of writing thesis essays. (p. 100)

FACE-TO-FACE PROMOTIVE INTERACTION

This is an essential element in cooperative learning as the students work together by encouraging one another, sharing ideas and resources, providing feedback, challenging each other's conclusions or assumptions to help reach the best conclusions and decisions, and demonstrating care for the other members.

INDIVIDUAL ACCOUNTABILITY

One or two members should not carry the group and let the others coast. Individual accountability can be facilitated through keeping the size of the group small, randomly calling on one of the group members to report on how the group is doing, observing group behaviour and individual participation in the group, and assigning one member the role of checker.

INTERPERSONAL AND SMALL-GROUP SKILLS

It is important that students learn to communicate and listen effectively, resolve conflicts when they arise, and support one another and the group process.

GROUP PROCESSING

This element focuses on examining how well the group has been working together. This can occur during the group task, where members step back and ask how they are doing as a group, and at the end, where there is a summative evaluation. Group members can simply ask what has been working well and where improvement is needed. Teachers can also give the group feedback on what they have observed.

The Johnsons stated that over 875 studies have been done demonstrating the positive effect of cooperative learning on student growth and achievement. It has also facilitated higher-level reasoning, more frequent generation of new ideas, and greater transfer of learning from one situation to another.

The School Community

This aspect of community will be discussed more fully in chapter 5, The Whole School. Simply put, the whole school is a place where teachers and students feel at home. They look forward to being there. The principal plays a central role in setting the tone of the school. Again, non-verbal behaviours (tone of voice and eye contact) are important in this process.

One principal commented how calmness is important to the whole process of change: 'To get any kind of change happening in schools, it's imperative that people are calm and are in an almost meditative state in order to make those changes that are being demanded.' This principal runs meetings that do not have an agenda: 'We're just here to talk about the work that we're doing, and enjoy each other.' She adds this is 'not team building, it's just kind of being together, it doesn't have a name.'

Ideally, the school should be a place that Martin Luther King, Jr, called The Beloved Community, which is a place of both love and justice. This vision and how it can be realized are discussed in the next chapter.

The Neighbourhood Community

The school should be an integral part of community life in which there is flow back and forth between school and community. This can involve members of the community coming to the school to share their expertise and tell interesting stories about the community or inviting an artist-in-residence to come to the school. It also involves students going into the community to be part of community life. Service learning involves students in community activities that are also linked to academic work in the school. Examples of service learning were cited in chapter 2.

The Global Community

Global education helps the students see themselves as part of the global community. Global education shares the same principles as holistic education, particularly with regard to the concept of interdependence. David Selby (2001) argues that holistic and global education are founded on the principle of radical interconnectedness, in which everything is in constant change. Selby believes that a connection between holistic education and global education is the need to recognize the importance of the inner journey and how this journey is closely linked to the outside world. He argues that the global/holistic curriculum should include the following strategies:

- cooperative, interactive learning
- children- (not child-) centred
- mixed-paced learning
- empathetic, embodied learning
- spiritual learning
- slow learning (p. 14)

Another important global educator is Robert Muller, who developed the concept of the World Core Curriculum (www.worldcorecurricu lum.org). This curriculum has four main components:

- our planetary home and our place in the universe
- our place in time
- the family of humanity
- the miracle of individual life

Several schools have implemented Muller's curriculum. The first one was established in 1979 in Arlington, Texas, and now functions as the centre for World Core Curriculum work.

Earth Connections

Whole child education and the ecology movement are closely linked through the concept of interdependence. Both share the principle that interconnectedness is a fundamental reality of nature and should guide our awareness and actions. The ecology movement can be traced to Thoreau, Muir, and others, but many feel it was the picture of the earth taken from the moon in 1968 that led to a deeper ecological awakening. We saw the beauty and mystery of the planet in space. For many people, this photograph led to a deeper love and reverence for the earth and concern for how it is being threatened by modern life.

Earth connections can reawaken us to the natural processes of life. The wind, the sun, the trees, and grass can help us be alive and awaken us. As much as possible, students should have direct experiences with the earth through such activities as gardening, caring for animals, and outdoor education.

Gardening

One example of this type learning is gardening. In their book *Digging Deeper*, Kiefer and Kemple (1998) describe how youth gardens can be integrated with schools and communities. They identify their vision at the beginning of the book:

> Growing gardens with children is a living testament to how to restore our ancient ties to the natural rhythms of the earth itself. It is in the learning of this lesson – flower by flower, child by child, season by season – that we will be able to reclaim the heritage that is rightfully ours: as the caretakers of a natural paradise where all species thrive. (p. xiii)

Kiefer and Kemple argue that growing a garden has several benefits for children:

- seeing the results of growing food with their own hands
- working in harmony with the forces of nature
- learning basic academic skills in science, math, language, and social studies
- learning to work cooperatively with others

The book is part of the 'Garden in Every School Campaign' that began in 1995 and has spread throughout North America. The process not only involves schools and children but includes 'elders to share their experience, stories and practical wisdom; local historians, naturalist, farmers, artisans and other professionals willing to contribute their expertise' (p. xiv) as well parents and families. To begin the project, the school should do a needs survey that looks at such questions as:

- What sites are available for a garden?
- Are there sources of funding?
- What organizations can assist?
- Are there already projects for young people in the community that involve gardening?

This survey can be done formally through questionnaires or informally through phone calls. After the needs survey, there is usually an organizing meeting. Kiefer and Kemple give detailed instructions for organizing such a meeting. Their book is also filled with case studies for each phase of the process. For example, they describe how San Antonio developed their program to become the 'Youth Garden Capital of America.' The leader of the work there is Vernon Mullens, who introduces young people to different types of gardens such as the 'Brains and Grains Garden,' the 'Dietcise Garden,' and the 'Melting Pot Garden.'

The next phase in the garden-building process is to develop a team. There should be a core 'all-weather team' that does the basic planning and work and a 'fair-weather team' that contributes to specific aspects of the project. The book is filled with practical information such as an hour-by-hour sample day in the garden. They suggest weekly themes; for example, for as soil theme, students could examine how soil nurtures the plants in the garden. Kiefer and Kemple describe how a project called The Village of Arts and Humanities in Philadelphia reclaimed parts of the city that had been abandoned and established eight community parks and gardens.

The third phase involves garden design. A couple of ideas for garden design include the *nutrition garden* and the *heritage garden*, which is based on approaches that have been used in the community over several generations.

The next phase includes identifying the appropriate site, tilling the soil, laying out the garden, and planting. The authors describe how a composter can be built.

The book also deals with issues of class and race, as some African-American families wonder why their children are doing work that was often a burden to their ancestors.

The authors suggest having an opening day ceremony when the ground is first broken. Once the process is started, students can keep a garden journal where they describe the plant growth as well as the weeds and insects that also inhabit the garden. Over the summer, activity shifts to watering, weeding, and mulching. In the fall, of course, is the harvest. Students can save seeds for planting next spring, make edible jewellery, and can, cook, or freeze the vegetables.

Finally, Kiefer and Kemple suggest extensive procedures for ongoing *assessment* of the project and then for a more summative *evaluation*. They include checklists and sample portfolio contents. Some of the items in the portfolio include student products, student affective surveys, anecdotal observations and reflections, participation graphs, community impact scrapbooks, and culminating activity surveys.

Body–Mind Connections

One example of fragmentation in modern life is the separation of body and mind. The whole curriculum seeks to restore this connection. Waldorf education uses eurythmy, a unique form of movement education. It is usually taught by a teacher trained in the field, but the classroom teacher is encouraged to take part in the lesson. Harwood (1958) suggests: 'When the eurythmy teacher is as much interested in what the children are learning in their main lessons as the class teacher in what they are doing in movement, the children thrive in a harmony of mind and will' (p. 154). In secondary schools, eurythmy can be combined with drama, 'perhaps in a play when there are nature spirits, as in Milton's *Comus*, or *A Midsummer Night's Dream*' (p. 155).

An ancient practice for connecting body and mind is yoga, which is being used more frequently in schools. One of my students, Nancy Zigrovic (2005), teaches at a secondary school in Oakville, Ontario, and uses both meditation and yoga with her students. She describes her experience with one class of grade 10 non-college-bound students:

I have also had the pleasure to work with a grade 10 Applied Canadian History class of twenty students, fourteen of whom are boys. Many of these students provide the quintessential example of discouraged learners – they are adolescents who often find the traditional classroom a very difficult place to be. They find it hard to focus and listen attentively, and are often described by teachers as 'behavioural problems.' However, from the first time that we tried both meditation and yoga together, they were receptive and open to new approaches. In our meditation, we began with short exercises in breathing and focus. They seemed at first reluctant to close their eyes in the presence of their peers; I explained that they could simply gaze downwards in front of them. When they could see that I felt comfortable in the classroom and had closed my eyes, all began to follow what I was modelling. Even in our first debriefing, they talked about how they liked being still for a few moments.

During my next and subsequent visits with the History class, we moved into a more physical form of hatha yoga, incorporating what we had already learned about breathing and focus. One of the initial responses from a boy in the class included, 'I thought that this yoga was pretty good. If we did it a little longer, it would probably be better. And once we get past the stage of laughing it would be good.' We did work at sustaining our practice for longer periods of time and the students became more comfortable with the various asanas as well as with making space for silence. Most importantly, however, they began to trust each other, and the hurtful comments that seemed to be a regular part of the classroom vernacular were becoming less frequent. In their latest reflection, not one student expressed concern about doing yoga or wished to not participate in the practice. I have been meeting with this particular class two times per week during the past two months, and some of their comments include:

At first when we were doing it, I didn't think it would really work, but after doing the exercises, I felt really relaxed and good. My favourite one would be the Namaste. It really makes me stretch and relieve stress. Thank you for doing it with us.

Another student wrote:

I like the yoga because it helps me concentrate a lot better because usually I can't concentrate very well. It also helps me calm down and focus on what I am doing.

And this student summarizes the soul connection:

This isn't the first time I've done yoga. We had to do this for hockey, before our championship game; our coach's wife used to be a yoga instructor. We ended up winning the championship game because we were all refreshed from our little yoga session. My opinion on yoga is it soothes the soul. (pp. 9–10)

There are many books that can help teachers introduce yoga into the classroom. Ellen Schwartz's (2003) book on yoga is a helpful guide for young people that has step-by-step instructions of how to do sixteen yoga poses. It also describes how these exercises can be modified for children with different disabilities.

Eurythmy and yoga are just some of the ways to connect body and mind. The goal of these methods is to assist in the *embodiment* of learning so that it does not remain a disconnected fact or an abstract concept but is integrated through our entire being

Thinking Connections

The whole curriculum focuses on holistic thinking, which links the analytic and intuitive. Einstein and Mozart are examples of individuals who were able to effectively relate both analysis and insight at the highest level. If our thinking is dominated by one mode, it is much less effective. If the emphasis is on linear, analytic thinking, we can become plodding in our approach and lose spontaneity in dealing with problems. If we stress the intuitive, then we can lose our ground. Our ideas can become irrelevant if we make no attempt to verify them. Generally, schools have not emphasized the teaching of thinking skills, and when they have, it has usually been linear problem solving rather than a more holistic approach.

A holistic model of creative thinking was developed by Graham Wallas (1926). The model combines both intuitive and analytical elements to make it holistic. Wallas describes four basic elements in the creative process. The first step is *preparation*, in which the individual gathers information relevant to the problem or project. In the second stage, *incubation*, the individual relaxes and does not make an effort to work consciously on the problem. Instead, it is suggested that the images realign themselves in the individual as he or she consciously attends to something else. In the *illumination* stage the solution will occur, often spontaneously and unexpectedly. The second and third stages, then, are the intuitive, while the first and fourth stages are more analytical. The fourth stage is *verification*, or *revision*, where the individual puts the idea into use and consciously works with it in a more detailed manner.

The Wallas model, and other models of creative thinking, are useful to the educator in balancing analysis and insight in classroom pedagogy. Visualization, meditation, and various aesthetic experiences can be used to enhance incubation and illumination, while logical problem-solving models can be used to facilitate preparation and verification. Effective thinking, then, involves both intuition and analysis.

With regard to classroom applications, the Wallas model might be employed in the following manner with regard to a creative writing exercise. First, the student focuses on the topic or issue and tries to achieve some clarity with regard to the problem. For example, students might be focusing on career choice. In the first phase, they examine the literature on career choices, particularly those careers that have initial appeal. In the second phase the students step away from the issue of career choice without jumping immediately to a conclusion and let the issue work through them. They sleep on it and let the unconscious work with it. The literature on soul suggests that careers need to be congruent with this deeper part of ourselves and so require patience and a contemplative approach (Moore, 1992). The period of time for incubation can vary greatly from one individual to another (for some the career path emerges in a matter of days, while for others it takes months and years). In assessing whether a job is appropriate from the soul's perspective, Thomas Moore (1992) raises the following questions:

> What is the spirit in this workplace? Will I be treated as a person here? Is there a feeling of community? Do people love their work? Is what we are doing and producing worth my commitment and long hours? Are there any moral problems in the job or workplace – making things detrimental to people or to the earth, taking excessive profits or contributing to racial and sexist oppression? (p. 281)

After the period of incubation we hope to arrive at an illumination. In this situation we can see ourselves in a particular career. This job seems to fit. The verification phase consists of the process of beginning to educate and train for this career. As we take courses or go through training programs, we test whether we have made a choice that is congruent with our soul or deeper sense of self.

Howard Gardner's (1983) work also has been important in broadening our conception of intelligence beyond what he calls logical mathematical intelligence and linguistic intelligence. The whole curriculum attempts to incorporate all the intelligences and to link them so that they are not used in isolation.

Andrew Johnson (2006), referring to Gardner's work, develops the concept of holistic intelligence (HI), which is the ability to solve problems in a way that nurtures self, others, and the environment. Johnson suggests that holistic intelligence can be developed in classrooms by introducing real-life problems that are 'mediated by values such as kindness, compassion, honesty, cooperation, integrity or fortitude' (p. 44).

Soul Connections

Within each person lies the divine spark, or soul; this is the mysterious energy that can give meaning to our lives. Nurturing the soul can also be called educating the heart, as Gandhi does in his definition of holistic education. The heart can be educated through what I have called a 'curriculum for the inner life' (Miller, 2000). A curriculum for the inner life can include visualization and meditation.

Beverly-Colleene Gaylean (1983) wrote a book that is filled with visualization activities for different subjects that allows for holistic thinking. She states that visualization has several benefits, as students

- are more attentive;
- enjoy the learning experience more;
- do more original and creative work;
- get along better with their classmates;
- feel more confident;
- are more relaxed;
- do better on tests. (p. 25)

With regard to the last result, Perlstein (2007) found that students were encouraged to visualize being calm and competent before taking the Maryland School Assessment Test (pp. 187–8).

One example of using visualization in science is to have students imagine magnetic fields around a transformer. The students can see themselves as electrons in the wire of the coil and experience the movement generated by the rapidly changing force field. Then the students can visualize themselves as electrons moving faster and faster as the two fields surrounding the coils interact and come closer.

Students can also use imagery in language and the social studies. In social studies the students could imagine themselves as a historical figure facing a particular choice and visualizing the thoughts and emotions that accompanied the decision.

Other subjects where visualization has been used successfully include mathematics (Arcavi, 2003; Wheatley, 1998), geography (Chatterjea, 1999), and reading instruction (Eisenwine, Fowler, & McKenzie, 2000).

Contemplation can play a role in the curriculum, particularly the use of mindfulness. Mindfulness means learning to be present in the moment, to be 'totally there.' This can involve first observing one's breath or simply bringing full attention to daily activities such as eating. An article in the *New York Times* (Brown, 2007) describes how mindfulness is being used in different schools. In a project at Piedmont Elementary School in Oakland, California, a 'mindful' coach visited classes twice a week for five weeks and introduced students to the basics of mindfulness practice. A Tibetan bowl was struck to begin and end each session. The project is being assessed by the psychology department at Stanford University. Dr Amy Saltzman, co-director of the mindfulness study at Stanford, said the initial findings showed increased control of attention and 'less negative internal chatter.' Another study of teenagers at Kaiser Permanente in San Jose, California, found that meditation techniques helped improve mood disorders, depression, and self-harming behaviours like anorexia and bulimia.

The Garrison Institute (2005) has surveyed many of the contemplation-based programs in the United States. One of these is the Education Initiative at the Mind Body Medical Institute (MBMI) at Harvard University. This program has introduced a technique called the relaxation response into the K–12 curriculum. The relaxation response includes the repetition of a word, sound, phrase, prayer, or muscular activity. Research shows that students exposed to this curriculum demonstrated multiple benefits, including:

- a higher grade point average;
- increased self-esteem;
- decreased psychological distress;
- less aggressive behaviour;

- better work habits;
- better attendance; and
- decreased unexcused tardiness. (p. 14)

David Forbes's Work on Meditation

One of the most interesting uses of contemplation can be found in the work of David Forbes (2005). Forbes, a professor at Brooklyn College/CUNY, has introduced meditation to high school football players. They come to his sessions because they believe that meditation practice will help them play football in the 'zone.' The zone is similar to Csikzment-mihalyi's concept of flow, in which the athlete is so deeply engaged in an activity that time seems to slow down and performance is often heightened. For example, the basketball player will make baskets in an almost unconscious way with little sense of self.

Forbes is also interested in how meditation can help young men overcome difficulties associated with male youth culture that can often emphasize aggressiveness, competitiveness, and homophobia. Meditation helps the person deal with problems rather than repressing them or acting them out. Forbes states: 'By creating space around a thought or self-concept, young people can more freely sit with their own experiences and become less attached to rigid, stereotypical notions of what one is supposed to think or who one is supposed to be' (p. 154).

Forbes offered sessions on meditation on a volunteer basis and approximately a dozen of the football players showed up. Most of the participants were African-American, Latino, Arab-American, and Italian-American. The sessions were held once a week and ran during the football season for a total of twelve weeks. In addition to the meditation practice, the students also had an opportunity to discuss issues that concerned them. Sometimes these discussions focused on football and sports and sometimes they centred on personal and social issues.

Forbes used a number of measures to assess the impact of the program. Generally, he found that 'some young men did evolve to more conscious, responsible, and self-reflective levels of awareness' (p. 164). Several of the young men reported that the practice helped them concentrate on the field. Forbes also noticed growth in the area of 'masculine identity development, such as being more mindful of how one relates to peers in aggressive and defensive ways and how one relates to young women, to one's self, and to something higher than one's own ego' (p. 164). According to Forbes, they became more mindful of their feelings and thus more responsible for their behaviour.

David Forbes has presented one of the most interesting and well-researched cases of the use of meditation with adolescents. His work makes an important contribution to the use of contemplation in educational settings.

Finally, I close this chapter with an example of how a math teacher used one minute of meditation in her classroom.

Just One Minute
by Naomi Baer

In a big inner-city public high school, in a Midwestern city, in my classroom, I start every class period with one minute of stillness. I am a mathematics teacher.

This began in the fall of 1997 with one particularly disruptive class. Out of not knowing how else to quiet things down, I started class one day talking about how we react to what goes on around us. We react to our friends, to the teachers, to each other. We react to the loud speakers, the classes next door, the commotion in the halls. We are bombarded by outside events. So I invited them to breathe in, straighten up the spine with feet flat on the floor, and be still for 60 seconds. Not to react to anything. I rang a bell, closed my eyes, and breathed. When one minute passed, I rang the bell again, breathed slowly, thanked them for the minute in which they gave their best, and invited them to thank those nearby. From this spontaneous response to one difficult class, I have continued to start all my classes in the same way. This is the fifth year.

In the beginning, it was questionable as to whether the practice made much of an impact on that disruptive class. Some students humored me and others ignored me, but for that one minute the noise level reduced at least a notch, so I continued. Over time, more students started thanking each other. First in jest, they playfully said to each other they would try better next time, and so it went.

I maintained the process, yet I never once made reference to meditation. I could do with my own minute what I chose without imposing anything on the students, and many days I practiced metta. About a month into the practice, in the middle of a lesson, there was a particular outburst from a student whom I had to escort out of the classroom. When we returned to the lesson, another loud student commanded, 'Ms. Baer, I think we need to do that minute thing again!' Vulnerable as I was, I closed my eyes in that class.

One day when I was delayed, a student spoke out, 'Let's marinate,' and rang the bells. Everyone did the one minute with him! From then on others wanted their turn to ring the bells. The noise and disturbances were reducing for the minute. The practice, however imperfect, gave even the most boisterous students a tool to use to settle the mind and body. I was convinced that it served not only me but the students as well.

In some of my advanced math classes, where discipline was not such an issue, there were mixed reactions. Most participated willingly in the minute of stillness, but a few were visibly uncomfortable and overtly resistant. I always thanked especially them for their minute of cooperation. Over time even these resistant ones became relaxed without having to work so hard at their resistance. It just was. A minute to do nothing.

This year one of my classes, mostly tenth graders, repeatedly requested to extend the minute of stillness even longer. So one day, with consent from everyone in the class, we did five minutes. When I rang the bell at the end, the stillness continued to linger. Wow! It was 'awesome.' They said they liked it when it was so quiet. They have continued to ask for more time, so we agreed to extend the minute on Fridays.

Our one minute has produced all sorts of responses. Once, a parent complained to the principal, who assured the parent it was appropriately secular if it came from me. Last spring as a student handed in his final exam before leaving for the summer, with tears of appreciation in his eyes, he thanked me for the daily minute. He said it meant a lot to him. This year three students from a class next door come daily to join my class for the minute, afterward thanking their buddies before returning to their own classroom. Parents of former students have come up to me in the grocery store to tell me how much their son or daughter appreciated that minute. They thanked me.

If nothing else, our 60 seconds has given me a degree more equanimity to start each class. That has been reason enough to continue. It was a huge challenge to accept the chaos in that first loud and disruptive class. But for just that one minute I told myself to let go of all my judgment – I am the responsible teacher, I have to keep order, it is my right and duty to judge and correct. I learned to accept just what is.

Over time the minute has softened me to my students. I have feelings of compassion for their being exactly where they are. Its authenticity comes across when I see little respectful responses, some thoughtfulness or a smile I would not have expected from them or from me. I continue to gain from our minute: to close my eyes and open my heart, to see the kindness that seeks an invitation to express itself from under the harsh exterior that circumstances have somehow created in my students. They show me myself. (Baer, 2003, p. 21)

Naomi refers to *metta*, which is a loving-kindness meditation. This meditation is described more fully in the next chapter.

Conclusion

The whole curriculum is *child-connecting* education. The teacher can start with any of the connections; the important factor is helping the child to see how many aspects of life are interdependent. The experience of one connection can open the door to seeing the interconnections in other areas of life.

References

Arcavi, A. (2003). The role of visual representations in the learning of mathematics. *Educational Studies in Mathematics, 52*: 215–41.

Baer, N. (2003). Just one minute. *Inquiring Mind. The Semiannual Journal of the Vipassana Community 20*(1), 21.

Beane, J. (1997). *Curriculum integration: Designing the core democratic education.* New York: Teachers College Press.

Brown, P.L. (2007, 16 June). In the classroom, a new focus on quieting the mind. *New York Times.* http://www.nytimes.com/2007/06/16/us/16mindful.html?_r=1.

Chatterjea, K. (1999). Use of visual images in the teaching of geography. *Geographical Education, 12*, 49–55.

Eisenwine, M., Fowler, E., & McKenzie, G. (2000, Winter). Visual memory and context cues in reading instruction. *Journal of Curriculum and Supervision, 15*, 170–4.

Esquith, R. (2007). *Teach like your hair's on fire.* New York: Viking.

Forbes, D. (2005). *Boyz 2 Buddhas: Counseling urban high school male athletes in the zone.* New York: Peter Lang.

Gardner, H. (1983). *Frames of mind: The theory of multiple intelligences.* New York: Basic Books.

Garrison Institute. (2005). *Contemplation and education.* Garrison, NY: Garrison Institute.

Gaylean, B. (1983). *Mindsight: Learning through imaging.* Healdsburg, CA: Centre for Integrative Learning.

Glasser, W. (1986). *Control theory in the classroom.* New York: Harper and Row.

Harwood, A.C. (1958). *The recovery of childhood: A study in the educational wok of Ruldolf Steiner.* Spring Valley, NY: Anthroposophic Press.

Johnson, A. (2006). Becoming full intelligent. *Encounter: Education for Meaning and Social Justice, 19*, 40–7.

Johnson, R.T., & Johnson, D.W. (1994). An overview of cooperative learning. In J. Thousand, A. Villa, & A. Nevin (Eds.), *Creativity and collaborative learning* (pp. 1–23). Baltimore: Brookes Press.

Kessler, R. (2000). *The soul education: Helping students find connection, compassion, and character at school.* Alexandria, VA: ASCD.

Kiefer, J., & Kemple, M. (1998). *Digging deeper: Integrating youth gardens into schools and communities.* Montpelier, VT: Common Roots Press.

Miller, J. (2000). *Education and the soul: Toward a spiritual curriculum.* Albany, NY: SUNY Press.

Miller, J. (2006). *Educating for wisdom and compassion: Creating conditions for timeless learning.* Thousand Oaks, CA: Corwin.

Moore, T. (1992). *Care of the soul: A guide for cultivating depth and sacredness in everyday life.* New York: Walker.

Noddings, N. (1992) *The challenge to care in schools: An alternative approach to education.* New York: Teachers College Press.

Perlstein, L. (2007). *Tested: One American school struggles to make the grade.* New York: Henry Holt.

Selby, D. (2001). The signature of the whole: Radical interconnectedness and its implications for global and environmental education. *Encounter, 14:* 5–16.

Singer, J. (1976, July). Fantasy, the foundation of serenity. *Psychology Today.*

Schwartz, E. (2003). *I love yoga: A guide for kids and teens.* Toronto: Tundra Books.

Wallas, G. (1926). *The art of imagination.* London: Watts.

Wheatley, G.H. (1998, Spring/Summer). Imagery and mathematics. *Focus on Learning Problems in Mathematics, 20:* 65–77.

Zigrovic, N. (2005). *Journey towards spirituality.* Unpublished manuscript.

CHAPTER FIVE

The Whole School[1]

The whole school fosters community both in the classroom and in the school. For me, the most powerful vision of community is Martin Luther King Jr.'s Beloved Community: a community of love and justice. In his earliest writing he referred to it; for example, during the Montgomery bus boycott he wrote that the goal is 'the creation of the beloved community' (1957, p. 30). The beloved community is a 'reformed and regenerated human society' (Smith & Zepp, 1998, p. 130). It is also a community based on interrelatedness. King (1963) believed that 'we are tied together in the single garment of destiny, caught in an inescapable network of mutuality' (p. 22). He saw humans as part of an interconnected whole. Each person owes a debt to others for survival and for the existence of society and should be aware that an injustice done to one person or group of people is an injustice to all human beings. King (1967) wrote: 'In a sense all life is interrelated. The agony of the poor impoverishes the rich; the betterment of the poor enriches the rich. We are inevitably our brother's keeper because we are our brother's brother. What affects one directly affects all indirectly' (p. 181).

King's (1968) vision was one not only of racial integration and but of universal justice for all human beings:

> Let us be dissatisfied until rat-infested, vermin-filled slums will be a thing of a dark past and every family will have a decent sanitary house in which to live. Let us be dissatisfied until the empty stomachs of Mississippi are filled and the idle industries of Appalachia are revitalized ... Let us be dissatisfied until our brothers of the Third world – Asia, Africa and Latin America – will be no longer be the victim of imperialist exploitation, but will be lifted from the long night of poverty, illiteracy and disease. (pp. 110–11)

Before he died, King spoke out against the Vietnam war and poverty in the United States. These concerns came from the broader sense of social justice. His objections to the Vietnam war led to his alienation from President Lyndon Johnson, who had previously supported King's civil rights work. Smith and Zepp (1998) write: 'King could not envision the Beloved Community apart from the alleviation of economic inequity and the achievement of economic justice ... King's version of the Beloved Community included all races, all classes, all ethnic groups, all nations and all religions' (p. 136). King's vision of the Beloved Community was also expressed in his famous 'I Have a Dream' speech in 1963.

The way to realize the Beloved Community is through non-violence. Non-violence for King was not just a strategy for change but a way of life rooted in love. In contrast, violence is based on hatred and usually leads to more violence. Only non-violence can stop this vicious cycle. This love and awareness must start from within the person.

King's commitment to non-violence can be traced back to the writings of Gandhi, Tolstoy, Thoreau, and Emerson. They all believed that the person must connect with the 'infinite within'; out of this connection arises love and justice. Gougeon (2007) concludes: 'Like Aristotle's "concord," such love is not only the glue that holds all of society together, but it is also the source of all social justice' (p. 177). This sentence catches the essence of the Beloved Community, as it must contain both love and justice. Without love the community becomes legalistic and lacking in human warmth, and without justice the community loses its sense of purpose and destiny.

bell hooks (2000) has argued for an ethic of love that includes 'care, affection, recognition, respect, commitment, and trust, as well as honest and open communication' (p. 5). This ethic should be central to our way of life in schools. This ethic needs to replace the current ethos of individual competition and achievement that our emphasis on testing has created in our education system. hooks argues that all great movements for social justice strongly emphasized a love ethic:

> The teachings about love offered by Fromm, King and Merton differ from much of today's writing. There is always an emphasis in their work on love as an active force that should lead us into greater communion with the world. In their work, loving practice is not aimed at simply giving an individual greater life satisfaction; it is extolled as the primary way we end domination and oppression. (p. 76)

hooks links love to spirituality: 'A commitment to spiritual life necessarily means we embrace the eternal principle that love is all, everything, our true destiny' (p. 77). I agree that love is our true destiny, and in this chapter I want to explore how we can bring love into education and our classrooms.

To create the Beloved Community we need to examine different forms of love and how they can be manifested in schools and classrooms. The rest of this chapter discusses six forms of love (self-love, love of family, love of friends, love of strangers, agape, and eros) and how they can be nourished in classrooms and schools. I am indebted to the work of Christopher Phillips, who describes the last five in his book *Socrates in Love*.

Self-Love

Love needs to start with ourselves. Unless we love ourselves, it is difficult to love others. Love of self means accepting ourselves, or making friends with ourselves. People from the East comment on how people in the West have a negative view of themselves, a lack of self-worth. For example, the Dalai Lama has commented that people in Asia do not seem to struggle with their identity. I have also noticed that children and young people in Asia do not seem as self-conscious as North American teenagers.

Emerson wrote this in the nineteenth century and it still applies today:

> These roses under my window make no reference to former roses or to better ones; they are for what they are; they exist with God to-day. There is no time to them. There is simply the rose; it is perfect in every moment of its existence. Before a leaf-bud has burst, its whole life acts; in the full-blown flower there is no more; in the leafless root there is no less. Its nature is satisfied and it satisfies nature in all moments alike. But man postpones or remembers; he does not live in the present, but with reverted eye laments the past, or, heedless of the riches that surround him, stands on tiptoe to foresee the future. He cannot be happy and strong until he too lives with nature in the present, above time. (p. 160)

One of several rationales for meditation is that it allows us to be in the present and thus make friends with ourselves. By being in the present, we related to what is happening now and not ruminating about what we did yesterday or worrying about what is going to happen to-morrow. This then is a reason to teach mindfulness to our students so that they can spend more of their lives in the present. Environmental education and activities such as gardening can also help young people see how they are part of the processes of the earth; this also lets them be more in the present.

Love of Family

This as an instinctive, natural form of love that arises spontaneously. The mother's love for her child is the best example of this instinctive love. Feeling the child in the womb, seeing the newborn, and caring for the helpless infant all contribute to this loving warmth that arises in the mother. The Roots of Empathy program described in chapter 2 is built on this form of love.

However, this love can go beyond the family, and when it does it is termed *ubuntu* in Africa. *Ubuntu* means that my well-being is the same as the well-being of the group or tribe; the two cannot be separated. Another way of saying this is that I cannot become all I can be unless I help you become all you can be. Nelson Mandela says that 'the spirit of *ubuntu* – that profound African sense that we are human only through the humanity of other human beings – is not a parochial phenomenon but has added globally to our common search for a better world' (cited in Phillips, 2007, p. 117). Nobel prize-winning Nigerian playwright Wole Soyinka stated that the world can learn much from the indigenous Africans' 'capacity to forgive,' which is based on a 'largeness of spirit' that is rooted in *ubuntu*.

Family love has been used as a metaphor for the classroom. Some teachers refer to creating a community in their classroom that is like a family. Waldorf education keeps students and teacher together from grades 1 to 8 to create a sense of family in the classroom. In public schools, in a process called *looping*, the teacher stays with a class for two or three years. As in the Waldorf school, this helps create a sense of family in the classroom.

Another method for creating a sense of family in the classroom is the classroom circle. The circle has its roots in indigenous cultures; for example, some First Nations people form a circle and pass the talking stick around to give each person a chance to share their thoughts and feelings. Black Elk said this about circles:

Everything the Power of the World does is done in a circle.

The sky is round, and I have heard that the earth is round like a ball, and so are all the stars. The wind, in its greatest power, whirls. Birds make their nests in circles, for theirs is the same religion as ours ... The life of a (person) is a circle from childhood to childhood, and it is in everything where power moves. (cited in Baldwin, 1994, p. 80)

The circle can be used in the classroom by giving each student a chance to speak. The circle can focus on a specific topic or have an open agenda.

I use the circle in all my classes for telling stories. I find it an exceptionally powerful way to share important student experiences in the classroom. For example, in my Spirituality in Education class I ask students to share a soulful experience from their own lives. As we go around, I am always moved by the students' stories, which have included experiences in nature, illness of a family member, and experiences with the arts.

Baldwin (1994) believes that the circle can be an agent of societal transformation. She describes a process called the PeerSpirit Circle. She makes reference to the work of Jeanne Gibbs (1994), who has developed the concept of tribes for use in classrooms. The tribe is a small classroom group of five or six children who work together throughout the school year. Gibbs also uses the large classroom circle to allow students to share events in their lives. Baldwin summarizes the work of Gibbs: 'Students in tribes have their contributions and feelings acknowledged throughout the process: they feel safe, they feel loyal, they feel loved and loving. In thousands of classrooms, the tribal community is preparing children to become adult citizens of the circle' (p. 159).

The school itself should feel like a family. There is plenty of evidence that small schools are more effective in promoting both academic and social development than large schools. Barker and his colleagues (1964) spent three years studying thirteen high schools in eastern Kansas. The schools ranged in size from 40 to 2,000 students and Barker focused on how size was related to student participation in athletics, class discussion, and extracurricular activities. In such activities as music, drama, journalism, and student government, participation was highest in the schools with enrolments between 61 and 150. With regard to classroom activities, the bigger school can offer more subjects, but the students in the larger schools participated in fewer classes and a smaller variety of classes than the students in smaller schools. In the music classes, which were studied in detail, Barker and Gump found that musical education and experience were more widely distributed in the small school.

Further research supports the finding that in small schools students actually do better academically (Cotton, 1996; Lee & Smith, 1994; Wasley, 2000). In reviewing studies that examine different institutions dealing with children, the World Health Organization concludes that institutions should be small, for example, no larger than 100 children. According to WHO, when organizations are larger than this, informal discipline based on personal contact is replaced by impersonal, institutional authority.

In general, North American school systems have focused on consolidation of programs and moved toward larger schools. For example, in the United States between 1950 and 1975 the average size of the elementary school rose from 153 to 405 students. At the same time violence and vandalism in schools skyrocketed. Of course, other factors in society have contributed to the violence in the schools, but it could be argued that the increasing size of the school has contributed to the trend of violence.

Larger schools are usually justified on the basis of economies of scale; that is, savings arise from joint administration and the use of one plant as opposed to several buildings. However, there are the costs of bussing, of bigger bureaucracies associated with larger school systems, and the social costs that can come from schools closing in small communities where the school is often integral to the social life of the town. Another supposed advantage of the larger school is efficiency. However, one study in Vermont (Sher, 1977) indicated that the larger schools were often less efficient because the administrations were more isolated from the community and the students. The same study indicated that in Vermont six of the top ten schools in percentage of graduates entering college were small schools (fewer than sixty in the graduating class) and that they were able to produce these results with operating costs, on a per pupil basis, of $225 less than the large schools.

Love of Friends

In ancient Greece *philia* referred to the love between friends. Philia also refers to the communal love that binds together a community. In Greece philia was essential to the formation of the polis, the basic civic unit. The Greeks saw the self and society as interconnected, and philia as one of the bonds that facilitated this connection. Phillips (2007) describes what philia meant to the Greeks: 'The philia cultivated among friends was meant to extend outward in widening circles – to neighbors, members of the community at large – until everyone in the country shared it, creating a sense of solidarity, loyalty, cooperation, and common cause' (p. 219).

Teachers can sometimes nurture philia in classrooms through small groups, or cooperative learning (see chapter 4). Bonds can develop between students that allow them to work together for a common goal. The film *Paperclips* describes how a classroom of grade 7 students in Kentucky focused on the Holocaust by collecting a paperclip for each person who was lost in the concentration camps. This project led to a strong sense of philia among the students and teacher. The service learning projects described in chapter 2 can also be used to create philia among students as they work together towards a common goal.

Love of Strangers

The concept of love of strangers was inspired by the ancient Greeks' notion of the gods, who they felt intervened in the lives of people. Thus, a stranger coming to one's door could be a god in the guise of a human. There was also a practical reason for extending friendship and hospitality to strangers: a traveller might expect the same generosity when he or she went away from home. We also find this tradition in India with the greeting 'Namaste,' which means 'I recognize the divine within you.' Some indigenous peoples, such as the Sioux, believe that there is really no such thing as a stranger because all beings, including animals, come from the womb of Mother Earth.

Today *global education* attempts to see all beings on the planets as connected and not as strangers. Schools have programs where students write to pen pals in other countries or communicate with them over the Internet. It could be argued that the Internet is helping create McLuhan's global village in which there are fewer strangers.

The practice of loving-kindness meditation is a way to practise sending love not only to our friends and family but to all beings on the planet. When students see that all humans want to avoid suffering and seek well-being and happiness, then we can feel a connection with all humanity.

The essence of this meditation is to centre ourselves first in the heart area and to contact a basic warmth there. After connecting with the heart, we then attempt to share this warmth and energy with others.

For example, one could use the following approach:

> May I be well, happy and peaceful.
> May my family be well, happy and peaceful.
> May my friends be well, happy and peaceful.
> May my neighbors be well, happy and peaceful.
> May my colleagues be well, happy and peaceful.
> May all people that I meet be well, happy and peaceful.
> May all beings on this planet be well, happy and peaceful.
> May all beings in this universe be well, happy, and peaceful.

This approach starts with those who are emotionally closest to us and then moves out from there. Another approach is to move out geographically:

> May I be well, happy and peaceful.
> May all beings in this room be well, happy and peaceful.
> May all beings in this building be well, happy and peaceful.
> May all beings in this neighborhood be well, happy and peaceful.
> May all beings in this town or city be well, happy and peaceful.
> May all beings in this region be well, happy and peaceful.
> May all beings on this continent be well, happy, and peaceful.
> May all beings in this hemisphere be well, happy, and peaceful.
> May all beings in this planet be well, happy and peaceful.
> May all beings everywhere be well, happy and peaceful.

The words can vary as you wish for wisdom and compassion in others.

When you are doing this mediation, it is also possible to visualize the people to whom you are sending these thoughts. I have started my university classes with this exercise for the past twenty years, and I find that it has added immeasurably to the tone and feel of the class. I wonder too how the world would be different if this meditation were done before business and government meetings. It does not require belief in any particular religion but is simply a wish for the well-being of others.

Several of my students have used it in their own lives. One student from Ghana likes to practise this meditation when sees people on the subway or the bus. 'When I see people around, or when I move in the traffic, it gives me the joy to meditate with those people ... at times, you see some sad faces when you immediately enter public transit, and you have to meditate and wish them all well.'

Another student from Panama used the meditation in a similar manner: 'When I see each person in the subway, I look at them and pray for them. And I see a brother and a sister, and a family everywhere.'

A teacher who works with students training to be teachers has attempted to integrate mindfulness and loving-kindness into his teaching. He says, 'I'm encouraging my classes to take joy in the tasks that not necessarily glamorous … and the whole loving-kindness notion is that any kind of direction you give is simply a suggestion in a loving way.'

Agape

Agape is love with no expectation of return or reciprocity. Nelson Mandela (1994) practised a form of agape in prison because he loved his guards, his oppressors:

> I always knew that deep down in every human heart, there is mercy and generosity. No one is born hating another person because of the colour of his skin, or his background, or his religion. People must learn to hate, and if they can learn to hate, they can be taught to love, for love comes more naturally to the human heart than its opposite. Even in the grimmest times in prison, when my comrades and I were pushed to our limits, I would see a glimmer of humanity in one of the guards, perhaps just for a second, but it was enough to reassure me and keep me going. Man's goodness is a flame that can be hidden but never extinguished. (p. 542)

Does agape have a role in education? In the film *Être et avoir* (To Be and to Have) the teacher's love approaches agape. This movie shows a teacher, Georges Lopez, in a small school in rural France in his last year of teaching. At first one is struck by the traditional form of teaching he employs; for example, he dictates readings to the students. However, he deals with every situation and students with total attention and care. One sixth-grade student, Nathalie, is so shy she is almost mute. At the end of the film she is sitting with the teacher on the steps of the school talking about how she will do in the new school next year. He explores her communication difficulties in the most gentle manner and suggests to her that if she wants she can visit him on Saturdays. The girl is trying to hold back her tears. This is one of the most moving scenes I have seen in any movie, much less in a movie about education. Yet it comes from the depth of the teacher's caring about this student. One film reviewer, Rob Thomas, summarizes my own feelings:

With his university goatee and stern gaze, Lopez at first seems like a strict taskmaster … But we quickly understand that Lopez is a great teacher in every sense of the word, drawing from infinite reserves of patience and respect as he instructs his pupils, never raising his voice, never talking down to even the youngest student … *His teaching is simply one of the purest expressions of love I've ever seen on film.* (my italics) (http://www.rottentomatoes.com/m/to_be_and_to_have/articles/1238605)

Lopez's strong, loving presence conveys what is really important in teaching. Agape cannot be 'taught' to students; it must come from the teacher's soul.

Eros or Universal Love

This is love that goes beyond the individual. Martin Luther King, Jr, described this love in the following way:

I have discovered that the highest good is love. This principle is at the centre of the cosmos. It is the great unifying force of life.

When I speak of love, I am speaking of that force which all the great religions have seen as the supreme unifying principle of life. Love is the key that unlocks the door which leads to the ultimate reality. (cited in Lin, 2006, p. xxii)

This form of love is something that we participate in; there is no object, rather it becomes part of a larger, universal force. It is beautifully described by David Duncan, a novelist and essayist:

When small things are done with love it's not a flawed you and me who does them: it's love. I have no faith in any political party, left, right, or centrist. I have boundless faith in love. In keeping with this faith, the only spiritually responsible way I know to be a citizen, artist, or activist in these strange times is by giving little or no thought to 'great things' such as saving the planet, achieving world peace, or stopping neocon greed. Great things tend to be undoable things. Whereas small things, lovingly done, are always within our reach. (cited in Hawken, 2007, p. 188)

As Duncan so poignantly states, love is beyond any individual. As teachers we need the same boundless faith. It is what can sustain us through the hard challenges of teaching.

Once in one of my classes students were asked to pass around a sheet and put their perceptions of what was happening in the class. One student wrote: 'There is a lot of love in this room.' This love was beyond any individual and was the larger love that Duncan speaks about. Students feel safe and affirmed when this love is present.

The whole school is a place where we want to be because we feel that we are loved there. The film *A Touch of Greatness*, which features the teaching of Albert Cullen, shows a reunion of students in Rye, New York, whom Cullen had taught forty years previously. The only black student in that class said that he felt loved when he was a student in Cullen's classroom. Isn't love the ultimate answer to racism?

Jonathan Kozol, in his book *Letters to a Young Teacher* (2007), believes that we do not need 'overblown vocabularies about hegemonic differences' but teachers who through 'love and their inherent sensibilities' cross racial divides and find 'graciousness and generosity awaiting them' (p. 203).

Aldous Huxley, who studied with many spiritual teachers, read widely, and wrote books on spirituality, said that what he learned most from his studies was simply to 'be kind.'

Originally the term *Eros* referred to an energy that brings harmony to the universe. Eros, then, is a passionate energy, or love, that can overcome divisions. Ideally the principal in the whole school can be a person who acts with Eros and thus helps build community. The following principles are helpful, I believe, for the principal in building the Beloved Community.

Vision is an important catalyst for change. It is important that the principal live the vision since she or he is crucial to its actualization. Vision is not a mission statement but a lived reality. This vision, of course, includes the whole child at its centre. The vision is implicit in the ongoing life of the school and comes from the hearts and minds of the people who work there. The deeper the integration between thought and action, the more powerful the effect on teachers. The vision should provide a sense of direction for the school and be open enough so that teachers can share in the vision and contribute to its development.

Vision is organic. The principal's vision is not dogmatic but is flexible and can grow or change with our understanding of the whole child. Many teachers have told me that their conception of holistic education keeps changing and evolving. Fundamental change occurs at the most basic level from inside out (Hunt, 1987); in other words, deep change comes from the heart. Long-lasting change occurs when we feel a deep congruence with holistic principles and begin to live and teach according to these principles. In short, there has to be some form of inner transformation for whole child education to work. It can never be mandated or imposed. I have seen this happen with hundreds of graduate students I have worked with. When the principal's work becomes an extension of her deepest values, it is often filled with a deep sense of joy and fulfilment.

Have a focus, but avoid detailed plans. A principal needs a vision but not a detailed plan. Plans end up being contrary to the flow of life and do not allow the principal and teachers to be open to the present moment. Of course, it is important to have priorities and focus; but when we go beyond this with lots of fixed roles and details, trouble starts. We know what happened to the Soviet Union and its five-year plans, and I believe that our education system is suffering a similar fate from too many plans, commissions, and task forces. A principal working with a living vision of the Beloved Community is worth more than any recommendation from a task force.

See the school as a living organism, not as factory. Here I would like to quote Peter Senge (1990):

> Many writers on organization have used the metaphor of 'organization as organism' to suggest an entirely different image for organizational control from that of the traditional authoritarian hierarchy. It is the image of local control – countless local decision-making processes that continually respond to changes, so as to maintain healthy conditions for stability and growth. (p. 293)

Whole child education, then, views the school as an organism and change as organic. Instead of seeing the school as a factory where people behave as if they are working on an assembly line, the school can be seen as a complex living organism that is evolving – changing through a sense of purpose, collaboration, and a deep sense of inner direction.

The primary focus in this whole process is the personal growth of the teacher. The next chapter focuses on how we can nourish the whole teacher.

Change is not linear. The school can best be seen as a complex set of interacting relationships. It is important to understand the sets of relationships that exist within a school as well as how the school is connected to the surrounding community. When we gain some understanding of these connections, we can bring this sensitivity into our awareness as we work with the staff or a group of teachers. For example, how the principal works with staff is an extremely important factor. If the principal has modelled collaboration, then the chances are much greater that significant change can occur.

Acknowledge the non-verbal or tacit dimension. I believe that most change occurs not through language but at a non-verbal, tacit level. The unspoken has the greatest power to influence the direction of change. For example, the silent example of a principal or group of teachers deeply committed to whole child education can do a great deal to create a climate for change. We have become slaves to slogans and jargon on implementation. If we begin to acknowledge the importance of space and silence, we awaken to the place from which language arises. When we acknowledge the tacit dimension, words take on a deeper meaning rather than just 'head talk' which fills our ears. In silence we notice our thoughts and actions and begin to witness their effect on ourselves and others. If change is tied solely to language and models, it is doomed; when it acknowledges the silent dimension, it begins to unfold in powerful and sometimes wondrous ways.

The principal must be committed to whole child education. The principal should support teachers in whole teaching and using the whole curriculum; if not, teachers will function alone or in small, isolated groups in schools. The principal can use teacher learning teams and help establish a cooperative environment among teachers in the school. The principal can do this by caring for the staff as the teacher cares for the student; in other words, the principal is fully *present* to the teachers. The principal asks the same questions of herself as she asks of the teachers. The principal takes risks and thus encourages risk taking in teachers; she encourages risk taking by being open and vulnerable.

The principal realizes that change is gradual and organic and thus approaches it from an ecological perspective. This means that interventions are made with an awareness of their possible effects. Narrow, mechanistic approaches to change are avoided because they do not recognize the interdependent nature of things. Thus, if the principal is establishing teacher learning teams, she gives thought to the possible effects to each team rather than hurriedly preparing the groupings. Strategies for professional growth that are not too threatening for staff are introduced. The principal intuitively senses what each teacher is prepared to do and what opportunities are appropriate for their growth.

Through the passion and energy of the principal, Eros can help bring the whole child school and the Beloved Community into being.

Summary

I have described several ways of helping build the Beloved Community in our schools. These include the following:

- Promote *small* schools.
- Use *looping*.
- Use the classroom circle.
- Engage in service projects that help students bond.
- Practise loving-kindness meditation.
- Engage in Global Education projects that help students connect with students from other countries.
- Develop a living vision that the principal embodies.
- Be aware of non-verbal messages and behaviours.
- Do small things with attention and love.

Martin Luther King's 'I have a dream' speech is constantly replayed and cited. The Beloved Community is really the essence of that dream and provides an inspiring vision for our schools. It is time this vision became a living reality through the creation of whole schools for the whole child.

Note

1 Portions of this chapter were adapted from John P. Miller, 'Eros and Education,' in M. Sousa et al. (eds.), *International Handbook of Education for Spirituality, Care and Wellbeing* (New York: Springer, 2009).

References

Baldwin, C. (1994). *Calling the circle: The first and future culture*. Newberg, OR: Swan-Raven and Co.

Barker, R.B., & Gump, P.V. (1964). *Big school, small school*. Palo Alto, CA: Stanford University Press.

Cotton, K. (1996). *Close-up #20. School improvement research series*. Portland, OR: Northwest Regional Educational Lab.

Gibbs, J. (1994). *Tribes: A new way of learning together*. Santa Rosa, CA: Centre Source Publications.

Gougeon, L. (2007). *Emerson and eros: The making of a cultural hero*. Albany, NY: State University of New York Press.

hooks, b. (2000). *All about love: New visions.* New York: HarperPerennial.

Hawken, P. (2007). *Blessed unrest.* New York: Viking.

Hunt, D.E. (1987). *Beginning with ourselves: In practice, theory and human affairs.* Toronto: OISE Press.

King, M.L., Jr. (1957). Facing the challenge of a new age. *Phylon, 18* (April).

King, M.L., Jr. (1963). The American dream. *The Negro History Bulletin, 31.*

King, M.L., Jr. (1967). *Where do we go from here: Chaos or community?* New York: Harper and Row.

King, M.L., Jr. (1968). Honoring Dr Du Bois. *Freedomways, 8*(2), 104–11.

Kozol, J. (2007). *Letters to a young teacher.* New York: Crown.

Lee, V., & Smith, J. (1994). *Effects of high school restructuring on size and achievement.* Madison, WI: National Centre for Organization and Restructuring of Schools.

Lin, J. (2006). *Love, peace, and wisdom in education: A vision for education in the 21st century.* Lanham, MD: Rowman and Littlefield Education.

Mandela, N. (1994). *Long walk to freedom.* Boston: Little, Brown.

Phillips, C. (2007). *Socrates in love: Philosophy for a passionate heart.* New York: W.W. Norton.

Senge, P. (1990). *The fifth discipline: The art and practice of the learning organization.* New York: Doubleday.

Sher, J.O. (1977). *Education in rural America.* Boulder, CO: Westview Press.

Smith, K.L., & Zepp, Jr, I.G. (1998). *Search for the beloved community: The thinking for Martin Luther King Jr.* Valley Forge, PA: Judson Press.

Wasley, P. (2000). *Small schools and the issue of scale.* New York: Bank Street College of Education.

CHAPTER SIX

The Whole Teacher

We need whole teachers to teach the whole child. Whole teachers practise patience, presence, caring, love, and humility. The whole teacher is also a lifelong learner who is humble enough to realize that the journey to being a whole teacher never ends. This chapter begins by discussing the qualities of the whole teacher and then suggests ways of nurturing these qualities through various practices including meditation and mindfulness.

Patience

We live in an impatient society. Consider the roadways that are filled with impatient drivers or the exasperated individuals we see waiting in lineups in the grocery store. We see impatience in our children, who are used to watching television shows and videos that are geared to short attention spans.

As teachers we need to cultivate patience. Children learn at different rates and in different ways. If we can be patient and not be reactive, learning and behaviour can change. Every teacher has experienced irritating behaviour in students, but if we do not react in a negative way there can be positive change. A young woman in one of my graduate courses seemed inattentive and missed some classes. I was somewhat irritated by her behaviour and felt that she was getting very little out of the course. However, she wrote in her final paper that she had an eating disorder and that the class had been a healing experience for her. Recently, a male student in one of my classes seemed frustrated and unhappy; yet when I told the class that I would not be teaching next year because of administrative commitments, he stated that he was upset that he could not take my class in the fall. In both cases I tried not to react to their initial behaviour and found that patience rather than reactivity was the best approach.

Meditation and mindfulness cultivate patience. When we sit quietly for twenty or thirty minutes, we learn to experience a range of emotions and thoughts without trying to change them. People say that meditation is boring, but learning to sit with and watch the boredom cultivates patience, which can carry over into our daily life and our teaching.

Presence

As much possible, we should be present in the classroom When students come to us and ask a question, they sense whether we are 'there.' I believe that more than anything students want our full, authentic presence, and through this presence the teacher connects with the students. Yet this is a real challenge in today's world and in the busyness of the classroom. We can get lost in our thoughts, and this hinders our presence.

If we recall the teachers that have had an impact on us, it is often not the material that they taught that we remember but their 'presence' that somehow touched us deeply. The Zen Roshi, Shunryu Suzuki, tells a wonderful story about the presence of a teacher. He was head of a temple in Japan and was looking for a kindergarten teacher for the temple school. He repeatedly tried to convince a woman to take the job but she refused. Finally he said to her, 'You don't have to do anything, just stand there.' When he said that, she accepted the position. He was convinced that her presence alone would make a difference in the lives of the children. Of course, teaching is not limited to presence but the skills and understandings that we bring to our work.

Emerson, in talking to teachers, emphasized the importance of presence in teaching:

> By your own act you teach the beholder how to do the practicable. According to the depth from which you draw your life, such is the depth not only of your strenuous effort, but of your manners and presence. The beautiful nature of the world has here blended your happiness with your power ... Consent yourself to be an organ of your highest thought, and lo! suddenly you put all men in your debt, and are the fountain of an energy that goes pulsing on with waves of benefit to the borders of society, to the circumference of things. (Jones, 1966, p. 227)

Caring

One way to demonstrate our presence is through caring. Nel Noddings (1992) has written extensively about caring in an educational context. She cites the research of Comer (1988), which found that the single greatest complaint of students is that teachers do not care. She describes caring as a state of consciousness of the carer (or 'one caring') that is characterized by engrossment and motivational displacement. Another term for engrossment is being completely attentive. Motivational displacement involves shifting our attention to the needs of the other. 'When we watch a small child tie her shoes, we can sometimes feel our own fingers move in a sympathetic reaction' (p. 16). In caring, the needs of others become prominent in our consciousness.

We start to demonstrate care by quickly learning the names of all our students and taking an interest in their lives. For example, if the student plays a sport or participates in drama we can ask how the game or play went. Caring is conveyed by non-verbal behaviour as well; a warm smile and direct eye contact can be as powerful as any spoken word.

Caring for subject matter and the teaching craft are also important. Students can sense our engagement with a topic as the tone of our voice can convey our interest in the subject matter. How we present the material is also indicative of caring; for example, is there a creative approach to teaching?

Love

Do we love our work as teachers? This fundamental question is crucial. Love for our work manifests itself in our enjoyment of the act of teaching. Most teachers have experienced what Annie Sullivan felt when she connected with her student, Helen Keller. 'My heart is singing for joy ... The light of understanding has shone in my little pupil's mind, and behold, all things are changed' (cited in Howe, 2003, p. 228).

Ideally, we need to put ourselves into our work in the way Emerson describes: 'When you do a thing, do it with all your might. Put your whole soul into it. Stamp it with your own personality ... Nothing great was every achieved without enthusiasm' (cited in Howe, 2003, p. 235). This enthusiasm is closely linked with love for our work. Of course, teaching presents endless challenges and disappointments, but love for our work carries us through the difficult times.

Love also manifests itself in wanting the best for our students. We want them to do well and become whole human beings.

Humility

As teachers we realize that learning never ends. We are constantly curious about the world, our subject matter, and about how children learn. Our curiosity should match the curiosity of the child. Through this curiosity we can see ourselves in the students. Sometimes when we take on a major learning project (e.g., learning a new language) we can feel how the students must feel in learning something new and difficult. This curiosity keeps us humble; we realize there is no end to the learning process.

We are also humbled by the fact that we never can fully know the results of our teaching. Sometimes we will hear from a student years after they were in our class about how much they learned. Yet this is an isolated incident and we can wonder about our effect on all the other students we worked with over the years. Clearly there is a mystery to teaching, and being aware of this mystery is truly humbling. Henry Adams wrote: 'A teacher affects eternity; he can never tell where his influence stops' (cited in Howe, 2003, p. 238).

Towards Wholeness

How can we cultivate patience, presence, care, love, and humility? I have been teaching meditation and mindfulness practice to teachers for twenty years and believe it is one path to being a whole teacher. I teach courses at the graduate level to experienced teachers and recently to students in our Initial Teacher Education program. To date, these courses have introduced approximately two thousand students to meditation practice. Only two students in twenty years have asked not to do the assignment. So far there has not been one student who has reported an overall negative experience with the practice during the course. Most of the students in the graduate courses are women (80 per cent) in their late 20s, 30s, or 40s. While most of the students come from Ontario, I have also taught students from Brazil, China, India, Indonesia, Iran, Italy, Jamaica, Lebanon, Japan, Kenya, Korea, Malta, Malaysia, and Somalia.

Meditation

Students are introduced to six different types of meditation: meditation on the breath, counting the breath, loving-kindness, mantra, movement (e.g., walking), visualization, and contemplation of poetry or sacred texts. These methods are described in detail in the Appendix. Some students work out their own forms and integrate meditation with their own spiritual and religious practice. Although sitting meditation is encouraged, some students do movement meditation. For example, one student swam every day, approaching swimming with mindful awareness. Whatever form students choose, meditation allows us to let go of the calculating mind and become open to the listening mind, resulting in a *relaxed alertness*.

Students are asked to meditate each day for six weeks. In the beginning they meditate for about ten to fifteen minutes a day, and by the end of the six weeks they are encouraged to meditate for twenty to thirty minutes. Students are required to keep a journal recording their experiences of the meditation process (e.g., concentration and focus, how the body is feeling, etc.). The journals also focus on how meditation has affected them. Some of the themes have included:

- greater permission to be alone and enjoy their own company
- improved listening capacities
- increased energy
- being less reactive to situations and generally experiencing greater calm and clarity

At the end of the process they write a reflective summary of the experience. Below is an excerpt from one of these summaries:

> I find it difficult to express how the meditation experience has been for me … I find it difficult to use language to describe what's happened to me over the course of the last few weeks … What amazed me the most was how concentrating intensely on loving-kindness and its implications for myself, my friends, my family my neighbors, my teachers, my colleagues, my acquaintances, the people who pass me on the street, the people who upset me, the people who participate and perpetuate structures that I oppose – that projecting loving-kindness to them resulted in a tangible concrete shift in my relationships – without my necessarily knowing, or intending it. We always think we have to 'do' something in order to effect change, without realizing that we are acting, we are effecting change by attuning to our self, to our capacity for compassion and understanding and reflection. Mindfulness practice, similarly, I do believe effects change. For me at least it enables me to pause a moment before I react, before I blindly go about responding or acknowledging as I walk through my daily experiences without every really needing to be there. I felt the effects –

I felt a shift – I felt it most when it would suddenly occur to me that I'm feeling good as a result of relating to people – and I don't mean my friends and family. I felt it most when I related to strangers, when I looked at them and saw them for the first time, when I thought about them as co-creators, as parts of myself ... What I mean is that ... it is a matter of my not seeing a distinction between myself and them.

Mindfulness

Besides sitting or movement meditation I introduce my students to mindfulness. Mindfulness means being present in the activities we perform from moment to moment. Zen master Susan Murphy (2006) describes mindfulness in this way:

> A most simple definition of mindful behaviour is paying attention. *This gives beauty to all things; they feel attended to.* Mindfulness practice is that one-pointed attention, the mind of being right here now, that is learned and refined on the meditation cushions and gradually extended into all the activity of your life – sleeping, waking, working, playing, eating drinking, cleaning, tending children, making love, giving birth, enduring illness, even dying. It is not endlessly effortful. Mindfulness actually has contained energy that is like a tiger lolling on a branch, missing nothing and deeply relaxed at once. (p. 19; my italics)

If we can give this sort of attention to our students, then something beautiful can happen.

Several students in my class have found mindfulness a powerful practice. One student made it the main practice in her home life. She began the practice because her husband commented once that it must be painful to listen to him. She resolved to listen completely to her husband and children when they spoke to her. About listening to her children she wrote: 'Each time that I stopped what I was doing to listen to them, they seemed surprised, and then delighted, that I had time for them.' After a week or so she noticed that the 'noise level in our house had diminished considerably ... I felt a calmness in our home that had not been there before.' She also attempted to be non-judgmental when people spoke to her. She quickly noticed that she often entered into conversations with expectations of what people were going to say. Letting go of these expectations and assumptions had a positive impact on her relationships with her husband and children.

Mindfulness practice also affected how one of my students, Astrid

De Cairos, approached her teaching. She integrated mindfulness into her teaching day:

> I began each day marvelling at the miracle of life, of falling asleep and awakening to a wondrous world. With this thought, I began my morning rituals. Thinking of my daily routines as rituals actually helped me in attaining a more aware state as I washed my face, took my shower, ate my breakfast, and walked (or drove) to work. Upon entering the school, I decided to go to my classroom first. I had previously been going into the office to sign in and say good morning, etc. but this took away from the oneness that I needed in my 'mindfulness' training. I ritualized all my tasks – walking up the stairs, putting the key into the classroom door, hanging up my coat etc. It was actually amazing how being mindful of these simple tasks allowed me to begin my day in a calm, clear, and less cluttered way. How many times had I come into this room, dumped my coat, hat, and mitts on my chair, ran to the photocopy room and back, spent another half-hour looking for the photocopying I had laid down somewhere, not to mention the frantic search for mitts when it was time go out on duty? Instead, I began to become aware of my mornings in the classroom, and in turn they became calm and focused.
>
> My favourite part of this pre-school ritual is writing the schedule on the board. My team teacher had tried to talk me out of this last June (she writes the daily schedule for each day on the sheets of chart paper and laminates them). At the time, I explained to her that writing the schedule on the board had many different purposes for me. The most important one was that it allowed me to centre myself in the classroom. I look back now on how intuitive I had been and I am amazed. Being mindful of this particular ritual has made me fully aware of the 'here' during the hectic day. I stand at the front of the room and feel the smooth texture of the chalk in my hands. I think about where I am and I observe my surroundings – the plants, the books, the desks, the children's slippers – I am, for the second time that day, amazed at the miracle of life.
>
> The day begins. I stand outside the classroom fully aware of each individual as they enter the room. I interact with them, I say hello, it feels good. This is new. Until now, I had never made it to the door when the children entered – I was always too busy! I try to maintain this sense of awareness – aware of my feelings (physical and emotional) and my reactions to the things that are happening 'now.' Of course, the craziness of the classroom day begins and it becomes more and more difficult to maintain this awareness as the day wears on. However, now instead of working

through recess, I take the time to visit with colleagues in the staff room. When I can, I take a walk down to the beach at lunch and look out across the lake, mindful of the beauty of the world around me. When the day ends, I recapture this mindful state and fully participate in the end-of-day ritual with my students. After the children have left, I sweep the floor, being mindful of my movements and the sound of the broom. I often begin by thinking that I am sweeping the day's events away and that I am focusing on the 'now' – the actual act of sweeping. The pleasure of being here, and being able to fully participate reminds me again of the miracle of life. (Miller, 2006, pp. 79–80)

Other teachers talked about how the process of being mindful brought a deeper awareness as they interacted with others. This teacher talked about the impact of mindfulness:

Mindfulness practice ... enables me to pause a moment before I react, before I blindly go about responding or acknowledging as I walk through my daily experiences without ever really needing to 'be' there ...

What I am now 'seeing' is that I don't want to 'get through' my days, I want to *experience* them. I do not want to walk blindly through my days, my relationships, my environment, or my life. Nor do I want the children of the world to walk blindly through their days, their relationships, their environment, or their lives.

One of the results of mindfulness practice is that teachers tend to be less reactive in the classroom. When a student's behaviour is challenging to the teacher, mindfulness helps the teacher process what is happening in a more spacious manner rather than immediately reacting. Often the immediate reaction can be something the teacher later regrets.

One teacher referred to an incident with her daughter and how being mindful helped her overcome her initial reactive behaviour:

The second area of intense learning pertains to mindfulness. I always prided myself on being a good listener. But often I was attending to or distracted by a variety of stimuli. My new awareness of this ability was very clear when I was engaged in a circular broken-record encounter with my nineteen-year-old daughter. I was frustrated with her for not studying enough in her university program. She had admitted to skipping classes and spending limited time in study. I had said, 'It's your life!' She was noticeably upset with me. I stopped. I saw how emotionally upset she was and I said, 'If you said that to me, I would feel very alone.' She looked at me, realized I had taken the time to understand her feelings, and she burst into tears and embraced me. I am going to endeavour to be truly mindful of myself and others.

Like the tiger on the branch that Susan Murphy describes, during the mindfulness practice we cultivate a state of *relaxed alertness*. Relaxation means that we avoid tension in the practice; instead we just settle in. Still we need to be alert. So mindfulness is a balanced state of relaxation and alertness. During the practice we move away from the *calculating* mind to the *listening* mind. All day we are usually planning something, then doing it, and finally evaluating what we did; most of this activity involves the calculating mind. With mindfulness we shift to the listening mind and we are not involved in this process of planning, doing, and evaluating. As much as possible we just *are*.

The rush and noise of our world make it difficult for us to be fully present. For example, we may try to relax by going for a walk; but we often take our problems with us on the walk. We don't really feel the air on our face, or look at the trees, or experience the warmth of the sun. Nature can be very healing, but our thoughts get in the way. At times our preoccupations and thoughts can be a barrier to the world.

Another example of how it is difficult to be mindful is when we try to do several things at once. At home I can be watching television, reading the paper, and trying to carry on a conversation with my wife. In our attempts to fit everything in, our consciousness becomes fragmented; our presence is diminished.

Another word for mindfulness is wholeheartedness. When we do something we enter into it completely. There are many simple exercises that we can do to be more present.

We can start our practice by focusing on doing one thing at a time. The whole experience of preparing a meal, eating, and doing the dishes can be done mindfully. For example, as you cut the tomato for the salad, just cut the tomato. Sometimes we can be so preoccupied that we can cut ourselves, rather than the tomato. Gradually, we find that by just cutting the tomato without the mind chatter is healing in itself. As we eat the meal, we can also focus our attention on the eating, chewing, and swallowing. Often we read the paper or watch TV while we eat our meals, and as a result, we taste very little. Finally, when you are doing the dishes, focus on the task. Feel the water as it cascades over your hands and over the dishes. Often we can hardly wait to finish one task so that we can do something else. For example, as I do the dishes my mind will be on the hockey game which is about to start on TV. As I watch the hockey game, my mind begins to drift to problems that I may face at work tomorrow. As we do one thing, our mind is on another; we seem to live in the future or in the past.

One master of mindfulness is Thich Nhat Hanh (1976), a Vietnamese Buddhist monk, who has written several books on mindfulness. He suggests a variety of exercises in mindfulness; here is one example:

A Slow Motion Bath
Allow yourself 30 to 45 minutes to take a bath. Don't hurry for even one second. From the moment you prepare the bath water to the moment you put on clean clothes, let every motion be light and slow. Be attentive of every movement. Place your attention to every part of your body, without discrimination or fear. Be mindful of each stream of water on your body. By the time you've finished, your mind should feel as peaceful and light as your body. Follow your breath. Think of yourself as being in a clean and fragrant lotus pond in the summer. (pp. 86–7)

I suggest that students start with very simple activities in developing mindfulness. Gradually they can then bring their attention to more complex situations. Mindfulness becomes a powerful way to carry our contemplative awareness into daily life. Deborah Schoeberlein (2009), in her book *Mindful Teaching and Teaching Mindfulness*, states that mindfulness for teachers results in the following benefits:

- Improves focus and awareness.
- Increases responsiveness to students' needs.
- Promotes emotional balance.
- Supports stress management and stress reduction.
- Supports healthy relationships at work and home.
- Enhances classroom climate.
- Supports overall well-being. (p. 9)

I have witnessed the same benefits. Mindfulness and contemplation are different from reflection. They do not ask the teacher to reflect on something but simply to *be* with the object. Teaching can move back and forth between mindfulness and reflection. Reflection allows us to step back to analyse what we have been doing; mindfulness and contemplation just let us be in the present moment. One way of looking at teaching is to see it as a movement back and forth between mindfulness and reflection. Both are essential to good teaching.

Research on Contemplative Practices

The physiological and psychological benefits of meditation are well documented. Murphy (1992, 1997) has summarized these benefits from over 1,300 studies. Some of the benefits include lowered heart rate, reduced blood pressure, heightened perception, increased empathy, anxiety reduction, relief from addiction, alleviation of pain, and improvements in memory and learning ability. Along with other changes such as improvements in diet and exercise, Dean Ornish (1998) has found that meditation is an important factor in reversing heart disease.

Roger Walsh (1999) has summarized some of the research on contemplative practices. He categorizes these practices under the label of Asian therapies and concludes: 'experimental evidence clearly demonstrates that Asian therapies can ameliorate a broad range of psychological and psychosomatic difficulties ... and enhance psychological growth and well-being' (p. 104). These therapies include practices such as meditation and visualization.

More recent studies have shown the effect of meditation on the brain. One Australian study (Carter et al., 2005) on Tibetan Buddhist monks found that meditation facilitated the subjects' skill in focusing and shifting attention. Smith (2009) in her review of this research concludes: 'These are attributes that would be invaluable for gauging how and when one might act, and for perceiving the effects of actions' (p. 98). Clearly, seeing the effects of one's actions is an important skill in classroom teaching.

Research on the use of contemplative practices in schools is much more limited. However, Gina Levete (1995) cites some studies that indicate the positive benefits of meditation for students. In one study, at a boys' school in the Middle East, secondary school students were split into two groups. The experimental groups meditated for the entire year on a daily basis. It was found that they performed better academically than the control group that did not meditate (p. 2). A recent study of African-American sixth grade students by the University of Michigan also found some interesting results. Students who did transcendental meditation reported increases in positive affectivity, self-esteem, and emotional competence (Gavin, 2003).

My own experience introducing meditation to teachers is congru-

ent with the findings of Murphy and Walsh. We carried out a qualitative study on teachers who have taken my courses in holistic education
(Miller and Nozawa, 2002). The study, described below, was conducted
as a follow-up on people who had done the meditation in one of the
courses. Twenty-one former students participated in the study. Some
had been meditating for seven years after taking the class; the average
was four years. They felt that the practice had a positive impact on their
personal and professional lives.

Effects of Meditation Practice

All the participants, except one, commented on the positive effects of
the practice on their personal and professional lives. They said they
were calmer:

> There is a sense of feeling more centered, more whole, calmer, more peace-
> ful, more contented, or grounded. (male teacher) (p. 185)

> I'm not as agitated ... or I'm not as arousable from the point of view that
> things don't bother me as much ... I feel calmer, I feel more ... this word
> centered keeps coming to mind. (female nursing professor) (p. 186)

Another teacher simply said, 'I don't remember the last time I raised
my voice.' She added that one of students told her, 'Miss, how come
you're so calm all the time?'
Another main effect noted by five participants was that they felt that
the meditation softened them or made them more gentle. One female
teacher who does walking meditation commented:

> It makes me gentle. And I also find that I'm feeling angry or upset about
> something, and then I walk, then by the end of the walk – it doesn't carry
> the same power over me anymore. (p. 186)

Five participants felt that the meditation had helped them with personal relationships. One female administrator commented: 'It affects
all your relationships. They're better. They're deeper.' A male consul-
tant found that people come to him for help. 'Well a lot of my friends,
they phone me for advice. I'm sort of like their counselor because you
get into that whole realm of awareness and meditation and looking at
things in perspective.'

One of the most interesting discoveries was the way four of the teachers integrated meditation into their teaching. I have not encouraged teachers to use it in the classroom but instead stressed the need to work on themselves. However, some of my students have felt comfortable in bringing it into their teaching. One teacher, who teaches grades 5 and 6 along with grade 8 drama, says:

> I've been doing it now since Jack's course, so I've been doing it for three years, with all the kids, especially in drama, the meditation's amazing, and they love it, they ask me now … They'll come in … and now my students ask me, 'Can we meditate, we're really hyper.' Or, 'Can we meditate before the test?' (p. 187)

This teacher asks the students to focus on breathing as a way to focus and relax. She also has them visualize going to the beach or lying on a cloud. She also integrates the visualization with her teaching so that if they are reading a novel in class she will have them imagine some aspect of the story. In their study of ancient civilizations she had them close their eyes and see the pyramids and feel sand blowing on their faces. She sees the impact in their art and poetry: 'I mean I've never seen such poetry. Just with more colourful vocabulary. Colourful words, colourful language.'

Another teacher at the high school had introduced meditation to approximately 1,500 students. She teaches in the Catholic system, and in seven years she has never received a complaint from a parent. She explains how she introduces meditation:

> I first create a very safe environment in my class, so people feel very comfortable … And then we get to a point where I'm saying, 'Now there's a different way to pray. Usually, in our tradition, we mean we need to talk to God, or to the Higher Spirit, but sometimes we need to sit and listen … So this is a form to connect with your spirit' … And I have my students journal as well. So I ask for journal reflections and they're very powerful. And now word gets around because people come to my class the first day and say, 'Are we going to meditate today?' (pp. 187–8)

Another individual who taught grades 4 to 8 in the Catholic system also introduced meditation to her students. Like the secondary school teacher, she connected the meditation to prayer. She found that if she missed a day of meditation the students would insist on doing it. She said that the supply teacher who took over her class told the principal that her classes were always very calm:

> And I'm not a very calm type of teacher. I'm a very active kind of teacher, and I have everybody doing different things ... But I'm sure it's meditation, I can't prove it, but I'm sure it's that thing that brings us together. And it connects – you connect on a different level, you know not just the intellectual. But you connect on a spiritual level and when we were like that in our classroom the supply teacher would notice: This is a very calm classroom. (p. 188)

The following are profiles of a former principal and a teacher who have practised meditation.

SALLY

Now retired, Sally was a principal at a public elementary school for four years when she took part in the study. A quarter of the school's population were special-needs students. She felt that 'the job of the principal is to reflect and that a principal should be calm, as once she loses it, everybody else has permission to lose it.'

She started meditation using a simple form of breathing when she felt stressed:

> When I move into a meditative state, I feel a little energy, or I feel something in my brain that happens in my body that happens. And I'm there. And I'm aware of this shift.

Three times a week she also practised reiki, a healing technique based on touch, which is a form of meditation for her. She first learned it in order to handle children who were out of control.

She describes herself as a very intense person, and the meditation helped soften the intensity. One person at another school said that she was just lighter and calmer. She works toward that softer and calmer nature in her role and tries to see things in terms of community. She based much of her work as principal on a holistic perspective. Sally comments: 'The issues of connections, balance, and inclusion and voice ... It's through those holistic education principles that I see the school, and how I see the teachers and the children.'

A teacher on the staff who practises meditation had a strong impact on Sally and the school. This teacher runs the junior division meeting and serves tea at the meetings. At these meetings there is an emphasis on simply being present. Says Sally:

> It always starts with a calmness, there is no agenda ... It's just being there and being together. It's not team-building, it's just kind of being together, it doesn't have a name ... I think the way that people treat each other is so important here. We adapt to change, and embrace change, we don't resist – we look for being present to everything.

Sally is convinced that mediation is important for leaders. She realizes how important it is for people to see that leaders can cope with difficult situations:

> It takes a long time for people to get calm, but they won't get calm if the leader isn't calm ... It makes you more creative in your problem-solving; for example, out-of-box thinking. And it makes you more equitable. You see the staff as real individuals, as real human beings.

She tries to get consensus with her staff rather than imposing a decision on the group. 'We just talk it out and see what they want to do ... We don't have to make a decision right away, and we let everybody be included.'

In her personal life, she feels that the meditation allowed her to cope with the heavy demands of being a mother of three, a wife, a graduate student, and a principal. It made a difference in softening her at home and in her personal life:

> My husband said to me on Saturday, 'You're really anxious, you should meditate' ... that's provided the balance for us in a relationship ... we kind of sort stuff out in terms of problem-solving in a gentler way within.

DIANE

Diane is from Panama, where she worked as a teacher for eleven years. In Canada she taught Spanish for four years and is also completing her graduate degree in the field of second-language acquisition and teaching.

Before meditation was introduced in the course, she was a very busy woman, running from one place to the other. She said that she never paid any attention to anything for more than fifteen minutes. Diane says: 'I even cry when I believe that I missed so much of my kids' time when they were babies. I don't really remember that well, because I was on the move all the time.'

Since taking the class, she has been meditating every day for twenty-five to thirty minutes, using visualization and breathing exercises, which she says, 'made a tremendous change in her life.' She feels the need to be mindful and to care about people, nature, and everything around her. She says that she now honours everything that gives her life and everything that lives. She says she has even learned to appreciate such things as how the air moves through her hair.

> The impact on me is very powerful. I remember one day I just watched my kids. I watched them sleeping, I observed them, for so long. I looked at their eyes, nose, hair ... they look like angels ... Sometimes I just sit down outside and look at the skies ... I remember that everything is grace.

She describes how mindfulness has affected her:

> I hear sounds that I never heard. I hear the animals, I listen to everything that is there, that I never paid attention to before. I touch and feel ... I know that I'm living and I don't have a word to express what this means to me really.

Diane talks about the change in her professional life as a teacher:

> And in the classrooms ... I'm not there just to give a lesson. I'm there to give love, and to care. And I know that they see me as more than a teacher now. They have a mother, friend, someone to trust them.

How she listens to others has also changed:

> I used to talk non-stop, not even listening to others ... I have learned to hear. I listen to my students. Now I know who has a grandfather here and who doesn't ... But it's so important for me now to just sit down with my students ... Whatever they want to tell, if it makes them feel good and relaxed.

Diane says that the transition from being a hectic to a peaceful woman was hard at the beginning, yet she kept the practice as she was convinced of its benefits. She does not regret the change at all as she thinks that she would have become sick if she had not changed.

Other Practices

There are many paths to wholeness. The ones I have just presented are the contemplative practices that I have been using with teachers for twenty years. It is the area in which I have the most experience and expertise. Body work such as yoga, tai chi, and qigong can also be very helpful. In my class on Spirituality in Education I present a range of practices within the framework of the various yogas. These yogas in-clude *Jnana* yoga, which focuses on inquiry and investigation, *Bhakti* yoga, which centres on love and devotion, *Karma* yoga, or the yoga of daily life, and finally *Raja* yoga, which includes specific exercises such as meditation and physical movement (e.g., tai chi). Below is the hand-out I give to students from which they can select one or two practices to engage in during the course.

Jnana Yoga

This yoga involves inquiry into the nature of ourselves and of experi-ence. Famous Jnana yogis include the Buddha, Socrates, Einstein, and Krishnamurti. Practices include:

• Reading and working with sacred texts or spiritual literature. For example, studying and exploring the Bible, the Tao te Ching, or the Koran. This does not involve a literal reading of these texts but an exploration of multiple meanings and how these meanings can be applied to your own life.
• Contemplative journal – identifying and recording contemplative events that occur in daily life.

Bhakti Yoga

• Gratitude journal
• Kything – the art of spiritual presence. Visualizing the presence of another person
• Pilgrimage
• Generosity practice
• Loving-kindness practice

Karma Yoga

• Taking care of someone (e.g., hospice work)

- Doing work without attachment to the results
- Conscious relationship, which involves deep listening, not being re-active, and forgiveness
- Mindfulness in daily life

Raja Yoga

- Hatha yoga, tai chi, qigong
- Meditation (breath, mantra, visualization, and walking)
- Silence

In one semester, several students read the Tao Te Ching. Each day they would read one of the pages and reflect on its meaning during the day. Many of the students had never encountered this work but found it helpful it in their daily life. The gratitude journal is another practice that is popular with students. At the end of the day students reflect on their lives and identify the aspects for which they are grateful. This has been one of the most frequently chosen practices.

Some students go on a short pilgrimage to a place that has meaning for them and keep a journal during the process. Often this is a place in nature. Other students choose someone in the family where there has been some difficulty. In conversations with that person they will focus on listening to that individual without reacting. Occasionally a student will choose to spend a day in silence as their practice. Silence has been the traditional support for spiritual practice.

What is important is to find some activity or practice that can help bring balance into our lives. I encourage students to a choose a practice that they can use on a daily basis. Practices such as gardening and knitting are also helpful in nurturing the listening mind. Ideally, it should not be done as a thing 'I have to do' but as something that ultimately brings a deep joy in our lives. I would say the true test of doing some practice is whether it deepens our compassion and our joy. I have seen this happen in many teachers' lives.

I close this chapter with the experiences of one teacher as she describes the impact of meditation and mindfulness practice on her teaching:

> With feedback from the instructor and through dialogue with classmates, I decided to stop trying so hard to 'do it right' and just be. Again I sense classroom connections here. As teachers we are so caught up with doing it right and covering the prescribed curriculum and attending meetings and

perpetuating fragmentation that we miss out on the simple act of *being*; that we fail to be fully present because our minds are caught up with what comes next and what we are supposed to accomplish. We teach as do-ers rather than be-ers.

I have discovered that as I come to understand more about the process of becoming mindful and present with my students and my colleagues, certain changes in my teaching practice have become evident. These strategies of mindfulness have seemed to evolve, not as much through a concerted, conscious effort, but because they have felt necessary and important as partners to the changes that I am experiencing within:

- To greet each student as they enter and to say good-bye as they leave – I station myself at the door to meet them with a smile and some kind of non-threatening touch.
- To practise Covey's Principles of Effective Leadership, particularly 'seeking first to understand, then to be understood' (this has become the very core of my 'discipline' philosophy).
- To look at each student as they speak (harder than it sounds!) and to do nothing else except listen (this has required some additional double-checking to ensure that everything is prepared before the students enter so that I don't need to prepare while they are there).
- To gather together in a circle at the carpet to discuss any conflicts or difficult issues that have arisen.
- To play quiet music as they read, write, or create artwork.
- To invest time in their lives outside of school: to attend a volleyball game or visit a church youth group.
- To share my own life with them: my friends, my family, my fears, my passions, my stories, as I have asked them to share theirs.
- To say I am sorry when I am wrong.

… in short, to know them, to ask the questions that might help them want to know themselves, and to know myself more that I might see them for who we are together, a web of breath and flesh and humanness without distinction of class, race or role.

… It was working with another teacher that I experienced the powerful process of creating a multicultural unit organically, our explorations slopping out over the edges of the prescribed curriculum as the interest of the students stretched our activities over days and weeks and across traditional subject boundaries. As we mixed paints to match our skin colours and shared the stories of our lives and our cultures, I found myself feeling like I knew my students more than I have known a class of students before. It occurred to me then that these strategies of mindful presence and valuing the Selves of my students are not merely 'nice ideas' for building unity in the classroom, but the very essence and root of what I long for in a teaching relationship. I see such a growing contrast between mindful presence and my usual spinning through the entertainment mode of a 'have fun and keep them busy' teaching style. It occurs to me now how very little I actually ever knew about the lives of my students outside the realm of academia. I had satisfied myself with coaching basketball and holding hands during yard duty, thinking this was what it means to know my students. Perhaps to some degree it is.

However, my thinking is expanding somewhat to stretch into a new sense of what it means to know someone, student or colleague, in a way that facilitates true and effective learning and growth. To teach from an intuitive source is to submit myself to an ocean of largeness of possibility that roars and flows with its own greatness and power quite outside the realm of my orchestration and planning and timing. It is to let go of the illusion of my own control and expertness, recognizing instead that to limit my students to the meagre feelings of my ego is to miss the hugeness and importance of authentic educative growth. I am reminded here of my earlier teaching days, furiously pouring over the little section on China in the Social Studies binder, pathetically planning what glorious reams of knowledge I might impart, only to realize with horror that two-thirds of my class were *born* there. Who do I think I am? Teaching from the ego is ultimately a crash-course in humiliation. It is only when I submit to the truth of my smallness as one who is learning and struggling along a humble growth road with these brothers and sisters who are my students that I come closest to teaching in truth.

... so crucial and authentic was the experience of 'teaching through living' with my students, that I have since found myself questioning the validity of some of my former practice. I am beginning to see my students and myself as ultimately one growing, changing organism continuing to become. I am only beginning this journey; there is so much that is new and unknown to me about the scope and breadth of holistic teaching and living. I only know that it is becoming my passion and perhaps my life-work to teach and to live from the fireside, to 'be quiet and listen and see what we hear.'

References

Carter, O.L., Presit, D.E., Callistemon, C., Ungerer, Y., Liu, G.B., & Pettigrew,

J.D. (2005). Meditation alters perceptual rivalry in Tibetan Buddhist monks. *Current Biology, 15*, 11.

Chadwick, D. (1999). *Crooked cucumber: The life and zen teaching of Shunryu Suzuki.* New York: Broadway Books.

Comer, J.P. (1988). Is parenting essential to good teaching? *NEA Today, 6*: 34–80.

Gavin, K. (2003, 6 June). U-M Health System statement: Transcendental meditation study. http://www.med.umich.edu/opm/newspage/2003/meditationstatement.htm.

Hanh, T.N. (1976). *The miracle of mindfulness! A manual on meditation.* Boston: Beacon Press.

Howe, R. (2003). *The quotable teacher.* Guilford, CT: Lyons Press.

Jones, H.W. (Ed.) (1966). *Emerson on education: Selections.* New York: Teachers College Press.

Levete, G. (1995). *Presenting the case for meditation in primary and secondary schools.* London: The Intralink Trust.

Miller, J. (1994). *The contemplative practitioner: Meditation in education and the professions.* Wesport, CT: Bergen and Garvey.

Miller, J. (2006). *Educating for wisdom and compassion: Creating conditions for timeless learning.* Thousand Oaks, CA: Corwin.

Miller, J., & Nozawa, A. (2002). Meditating teachers: A qualitative study. *Journal of Inservice Education, 28*, 179–92.

Murphy, M. (1992). *The future of the body: Explorations into the further evolution of human nature.* New York: Jeremy Tarcher.

Murphy, M., & Donovan, S. (1997). *The physical and psychological effects of meditation.* Sausalito, CA: Institute of Noetic Sciences.

Noddings, N. (1992). *The challenge to care in schools: An alternative approach to education..* New York: Teachers College Press.

Ornish, D. (1998). *Love and survival: The scientific basis for the healing power of intimacy.* New York: HarperCollins.

Schoeberlein, D. (2009). *Mindful teaching and teaching mindfulness: A guide for anyone who teaches anything.* Boston: Wisdom.

Smith, S.E. (2009). *To be wise and kind: A Buddhist community engagement with Victorian state primary schools.* Unpublished doctoral thesis, Victoria University, Australia.

Walsh, R. (1999). *Essential spirituality.* New York: John Wiley.

CHAPTER SEVEN

The Whole Child School[1]

In June 2007 I was approached by a group of teachers and parents who were applying to the Toronto District School Board (TDSB) to start up an alternative school called the Whole Child School (WCS). They were working on a proposal to begin an elementary school with a holistic approach to education. They asked me to help set up an advisory committee that would provide support and guidance to their project. The school opened in the fall of 2009 as a K–5 school with an enrolment of 150 students and plans to expand to grade 8.

The Whole Child School includes many of the elements of whole child education that are described in this book. For example, they have adopted the whole curriculum as a frame for program planning. In their proposal to the Board they also emphasized elements of whole teaching (e.g., transmission, transaction, and transformation). In this chapter I will describe the development and framework for the school. Much of the material cited here is available on the school's website, www.wholechildschool.ca, and I encourage the reader to consult that site for updates.

The Rationale for the Whole Child School

The proposal for the Whole Child School (2007) refers to the Association for Supervision and Curriculum Development (ASCD) and their emphasis on whole child education. ASCD's commission on the whole child is cited in the school's rationale:

Educators and the public have long agreed that education must both include and go well beyond the academics of reading, writing, and mathe-

matics. Yet for our educational system and communities to develop whole
children, we must act, not talk; act in fundamentally different, not margin-
ally different ways; and act as schools, communities, and nations to ensure
a deservedly brighter future for our children.

We are calling for a simple change that will have radical implications:
put the child at the centre of decision making and allocate resources –
time, space, and human – to ensure each child's success. We call for a shift
in how schools and communities look at young people's learning. Lay
aside the perennial battles for resources and instead align those resources
in support of the whole child. (p. 7)

The objectives for the Whole Child School stated in the proposal included:

1. To nurture, inspire, and educate the whole child.
2. To establish a holistic alternative public school offering kinder-
    garten to grade 8 (graduated start with grade 6 in first year, grade
    7 in second year, and grade 8 in third year) in Toronto-Danforth,
    Ward 15, for September 2008.
3. To found a landmark public holistic school within Canada. To
    create a prototype elementary school that becomes a leading bench-
    mark for public holistic education.
4. To directly respond to ASCD's priority of focus on the whole child
    and fulfil the overwhelming community demand among TDSB
    parents and students for a public school dedicated to holistic edu-
    cation.

I would note the third objective that focuses not just on the school
itself but on its potential as a catalyst for change in public education.
To achieve these objectives, the proposal focuses on four main areas:
vision, governance, curriculum, and community.

Vision

In creating a vision for the school the proposal cites a passage from my
book *The Holistic Curriculum* (Miller, 2007):

   We care about children. We care about their academic work. We want
   them to see the unity of knowledge. We want students to see how subjects
   relate to one another and to the students themselves. We find that the

arts, or more generally an artistic sense, can facilitate connections between subjects.

We care about how children think, and in particular, we try to encourage creative thinking. We want the students to be able to solve problems and use both analytical and intuitive thinking in the process.

We care about the physical development of the student. We devote part of the curriculum to activities that foster healthy bodies so they feel 'at home' with themselves.

We care about how students relate to others and to the community at large. We focus on communication skills, and as the students develop we encourage them to use these skills in a variety of community settings. We encourage the community to come to the school, particularly artists who can inspire students' aesthetic sense.

Most of all, we care about the students' being. We realize that the final contribution that they make to this planet will be from the deepest part of their being and not just from the skills we teach them. We can try to foster the spiritual growth of the student by working on ourselves as teachers, parents, and community to become more conscious and caring. By working on ourselves, we hope to foster in our students a deep sense of connectedness within themselves and to other beings on this planet. (p. 12)

Governance

The Whole Child School works within the framework of the Ontario Ministry of Education and the Toronto District School Board. Within this framework, an Organizing Committee for the Whole Child School was established to guide the initial development of the school prior to its launch. Also important to the process was the establishment of an advisory board that would provide support and leadership to the process of setting up the school. One of the specific purposes was to 'provide thought leadership and practical guidance on matters related to *whole teaching* and advice with respect to appropriate instructional approaches and how individual teachers can adapt them into their own rhythms, inclinations and subject matter' (p. 16; my italics). The board was also to provide 'thought leadership and guidance on matters related to the holistic curriculum' (Whole Child School, 2007, p. 16).

As indicated above, I was asked to help identify individuals who would sit on this advisory committee, which initially consisted of twelve members. The committee included individuals working in Waldorf education, Montessori education, private holistic schools operating in the Greater Toronto Area, as well as teachers from the Toronto School Board and academics from the Ontario Institute for Studies in Education at the University of Toronto, Ryerson University, and York University. This committee met once a month from September 2007 to June 2009 and worked under the guidelines set out in the original proposal. With the school beginning in the fall of 2009, the advisory committee was replaced by an independent 'independent learning team' that focused on supporting the teachers as they began their work and setting a framework for assessing the success of the school in achieving its goals. Some of the specific activities for this team include:

- To support our WCS teachers in their ongoing inquiry into the question: 'What does it mean to be a holistic educator?' (Teacher as learner)
- To create a continuing forum where WCS teachers have an opportunity to describe and share their learning process as holistic educators and to access advice and counsel on how best to address emerging classroom requirements.
- To identify the strengths and weaknesses of the initial version of the holistic program and to identify program improvements – particularly improvements that are supported by research and evidence-based practices.
- To implement our operational commitment to research and evidence-based practices and their transfer into the holistic program. (Davies, 2009)

This team will also work with the teachers to develop a set of standards by which the holistic program can be evaluated. The purpose of this process is to maintain the original vision of the school and to prepare the program for transfer into the broader public system.

Curriculum

Originally the organizing and curriculum committees looked at Waldorf education as a primary framework for the Whole Child School. However, the committee felt that other holistic pedagogies should also be included. The proposal (2007) states:

It was at this juncture that we began discussions with Jack Miller regarding the use of his book, *The Holistic Curriculum*, and forging a formal relationship in support of Whole Child School. *The Holistic Curriculum* provides an excellent curriculum framework, combining the best practices of numerous approaches, and is an ideal template for the development of a holistic curriculum specific to Whole Child School. (p. 21)

The most recent version of the whole curriculum can be found on the school website under the link Holistic Curriculum, which describes the six connections – community, earth, inner, body-mind, subject, intution/inquiry – and how they will be developed in the primary and junior divisions. They have substituted the terms Inner Connections for Soul Connections. See the Appendix for how the proposal adapted whole teaching and the whole curriculum to the needs of the Whole Child School.

The following is material from the website describing the holistic curriculum:

Community Connections

Building a community starts in the classroom and extends to local and global communities. Through our community-building program, students gain skills to create solutions to difficult social problems. It is our hope that students who graduate from our school will feel empowered to take social action and will work towards creating a more equitable and just world.

The **classroom** is the child's first experience of community. The teachers at the Whole Child School (WCS) are committed to building a cohesive classroom community. To build community in the classroom, we have adopted a school-wide community-building program that provides classroom routines and rituals, as well as a common language. Some of the elements of this program are weekly classroom meetings, language for conflict resolution, cooperative/collaborative learning activities, and classroom discussions on building respectful relationships.

The students learn about **social justice** through our Social Studies program. Our goal is to introduce the children to multiple perspectives and to nurture empathy around social issues in the classroom that extend to local and global communities. This program is largely taught through literature, and teachers provide learning activities, such as role-play or inquiry, to connect stories to children's lives and experiences.

In the older grades, learning about social justice transforms into **social action**. In grade 5, teachers train peer mediation and leadership to students. Grade 5 students learn about school governance as part of a unit about Government. They take leadership roles in the school community. Throughout the year, they work with primary school students to help build a collaborative and cohesive community. In grades 6 to 8, students learn about **social action** and **justice** in the **local** and **global communities** through project-based learning activities.

A deep sense of school community or **sanctuary** will be created throughout the school. In a sanctuary, teachers and students look forward to being at school, as they feel nourished by the environment, which is one of respect, caring, and, occasionally, reverence.

Earth Connections

Students awake to the natural processes of life by connecting to the earth. The curriculum teaches students not only about environmental problem solving, but more importantly, how we are fundamentally embedded in the earth's natural processes. Our environmental program follows a similar format as our community-building program. In the early years, students develop a strong connection and relationship to the earth, and in the older grades, children learn how to take action. Again, the goal is to teach students how to feel empowered to take action and how to make sustainable choices about the environment.

A focus in the primary years is to develop a strong **connection to the earth** through our **gardening** and **farming programs**. On site is a school garden, and the students also tend a local community garden. The school has formed a partnership with a local organic farm, which we visit throughout the year.

Primary students go on **guided nature walks** to local conservation areas, such as the Leslie Spit and the Humber River. On the hikes, students hear stories and learn names of native plants. The children observe life cycles of wildlife – the migration of birds at the Leslie Spit or of salmon in the Humber River.

. In the primary years, we aim to teach most of the **Science curriculum** outdoors. For example, the grade 1 Science unit on the needs and characteristics of livings things easily lends itself to being taught outdoors. In grade 3, when the children learn about soil, they draw from their experiences in gardening and farming. Also, some of the **Math curriculum** will be taught outside. For example, students learn how to count when they plant seeds and learn about measurement when spacing the seeds.

From grades 3 to 6, the students will learn about our **relationship to the earth** and the natural resources we use in our lives. For instance, our Textile unit starts in grade 3, when the students learn about Canadian pioneers and learn how to make wool. In grade 5, the Textile unit continues when they learn about ancient civilizations. The students study how textiles are made and they experience how to make fabric from flax and other natural materials. The last part of the Textile unit focuses on **sustainable textiles.**

Grade 7 students choose an **environmental action project** for the year. They document what environmental action they have taken, how their work has made a contribution, and what they would like to do in the future. The goal is for the children to discover what actions, even small ones, that they can take to improve the environment. A student may focus on sustainable modes of transportation and an action that the student can start to promote more sustainable transportation.

Inner Connections

A holistic curriculum connects students with their inner lives, which is defined here as a vital and mysterious energy that gives meaning and purpose to one's life. Connections to students' inner lives are nourished through **storytelling.** Stories that are told verbally (not read from a book) capture children's imaginations. It is a sacred moment in the day when a teacher tells a story from his or her head, without prompts. Students fall silent as they wait to hear the next part of the story from the day before. Myths, legends, folktales, sage stories, fairytales, histories from around the world are told to the children throughout the grades to connect students to our diverse, cultural heritages and to old knowledge that has been passed down through every culture.

Some examples of classroom routines and rituals that connect students with their souls are: **singing** and **recitation** of poems on a daily basis; **meditation** and **visualization** practices; **community talking circle**, during which each student has an opportunity to share; and **circle time**, which includes singing, dancing, and movement activities.

The school comes together to celebrate seasonal festivals and auspicious dates throughout the year. **School-wide celebrations** have ritual and ceremonial elements to them, creating connections as a school and creating feelings that are usually associated with being in a sanctuary.

Body–Mind Connections

The curriculum emphasizes a natural connection between body and mind. Students are encouraged to explore the connections between their body and emotions, and to develop a sense of what their bodies have to say. A priority is placed on healthy, positive communication and mindfulness in all actions – being aware of what one is doing while doing it. Mindfulness and a focus on breath encourage students to slow down and be present with one task at a time.

Techniques employed to stimulate the mind-body connection in the classroom include drama, creative movement, dance, performance, role-play, yoga, meditation, and relaxation.

Subject Connections

A connection is made between school subjects at WCS, producing an integrated curriculum. This occurs on a number of levels, with a strong focus on **transdisciplinary** teaching, when several subjects are integrated around a broad theme. Usually, teachers make subject connections during the **morning lesson**.

The year is divided into ten to twelve three- to four-week lesson blocks. One subject is the focus of the lesson block, and a number of other subjects are integrated into the lesson theme. For example, in the primary grades literacy is usually integrated into a Math lesson block through stories, poems, and math journals. In the upper grades, Math and Language Arts are integrated into Science, Social Studies, Geography, or History lesson blocks. The consistent study of one subject helps to deepen the students' understanding of the subject.

Intuition and Inquiry Connections

An **inquiry-based** approach is one of the ways in which teachers develop students' intuition. At WCS, teachers provide activities that facilitate exploration in the playground, in nature, and in the classroom. Students direct the exploration, making discoveries and predictions as the teacher encourages with open-ended questions. For example, a teacher tells students to observe where plants like to grow. Inquiry-based questions connected to this observation might be: 'Where did you see ferns growing?' and 'Why do ferns grow in those areas?' The teacher documents the students' discussions and explorations.

Children may choose to document their explorations through drawings, writing, mixed-media art forms, and music. The teacher provides students with recyclables, wire, clay, paint, and other materials (Reggio Emilia inspires this approach).

Community

The Whole Child School is a school within a school – Roden Public

School in the east end of Toronto – and occupies the third floor of this school. I was at the school on a cold night in February when registration began. The gym was packed with parents and children. In that first week there were 320 applications for 160 spaces so that eventually a lottery was used to select the incoming students. In a letter to the advisory board in June 2009 Stephen Davies, the administrative co-leader of the project, wrote about 'the strength and commitment of our parent community that has sustained our initiative for the last two and a half years, and continues to re-energize our volunteer base with a wealth of talented and passionate parents.'

I agree with the following statements from the summary section of the proposal (2007) for the Whole Child School:

> Whole Child School has the potential to be a leading prototype school within the Toronto District School Board. We possess all the key cornerstones for the success of a school: a strong, clear vision that resonates with our communities, a governance model backed by solid industry expertise, a curriculum geared specifically to our school, and tremendous support from all stakeholders in our community.
>
> The concept for Whole Child School belongs in the public school system. Holistic education is no longer a niche interest – it is for every child, everywhere. The largest professional association of educators in the world has identified holistic education as their top priority – evidence that the mainstream has embraced this fully. Whole Child School is perfectly timed to bridge the emerging theory and the community demand to create an exemplary school. (p. 34)

The Whole Child School opened its doors on Tuesday, 8 September 2009. It is the school of choice for over 150 students drawn from over ninety families. For the 2009–10 school year there were three combined Junior Kindergarten and Senior Kindergarten classes, a grade 1 class, a grade 2 class, a grade 3 class, and a split grade 4/5 class.

In the first year the staff has drawn on a number of holistic approaches in their curriculum initiatives. For example, primary teachers have begun integrating the Montessori math approach into the program. This approach provides the children with a strong foundation in whole numbers. Storytelling, based mostly on Waldorf methods, has been a central part of the language curriculum.

Outdoor education and environmental education have also been central to the WCS curriculum. Much of the Kindergarten program has been held outdoors so that the children can be in touch with nature. For the whole school, one afternoon per week has been dedicated to outdoor education as teachers, parents, and children can go hiking, skating, gardening, or farming. The staff has started to work with an organization called the PINE project (www.pineproject.org) to augment their environmental program. WCS has joined with Roden School in pursuing the eco-schools certification. An initial waste audit was completed in the fall and a follow-up audit is planned for the spring. The vice principal, Marc Sprack, has been very supportive of these efforts and has championed the Environment Club as a key joint club between WCS and Roden schools.

WCS is the largest of the four new alternative schools in the Toronto District School Board. Teresa Tafaro, principal of both WCS and Roden, has been an important ally in establishing and operationalizing WCS from an administrative standpoint. She assisted the founding parent body as they became the executive for the new WCS School Council and has worked collaboratively with the School Council and WCS Teaching Team to establish functional working relationships that can enable WCS to fulfil its vision. WCS is blessed to have an active and involved parent community with rich and varied talents.

Stephen Davies has chaired the Independent Learning Team, which consists of holistic educators who provide support to the teachers and is exploring a research program for WCS. This group, which meets approximately every six weeks, has included WCS teachers in the meetings. Several individuals on the ILT have worked with teachers to provide instructional support. For example, my graduate assistant, Jennifer Motha, and I have conducted sessions on how the teachers can employ mindfulness and visualization techniques in the classroom.

Starting a new school is a tremendous undertaking. I close with comments from Stephen Davies:

The WCS Teaching Team has had a challenging and rewarding year. The individual commitment of the WCS teachers to implementing the holistic program has been awesome. All of the teachers have worked tirelessly to design and deliver instructional blocks and individual lesson plans that animate the principles of holistic education and thematically connect the Ontario Curriculum. The heroic effort put out by the teachers has been driven by their personal passion to be the best holistic educators they can be. And the work is paying off. There has been very positive feedback from the majority of the parent community about the extent to which their children love coming to school.

Note

1   The Whole Child School community is changing the name of the school. The reason for the change is that as the school expands to include older students in the higher grades these classes will include young adolescents who may not feel comfortable with the word 'child' as part of the school's name. Names being considered as this book was in the production process included Ashdale Holistic School, Four Pines Holistic School, and Terra Holistic School.

References

Davies, S. (2009, 15 June). Personal communication to advisory board.

Miller, J. (2007). *The holistic curriculum*, 2nd ed. Toronto: University of Toronto Press.

Whole Child School (2007, 30 September). Whole Child School: Proposal for an alternative elementary school. www.wholechildschool.ca.

The Holistic Curriculum. www.wholechildschool.ca.

Meditation Instructions

This appendix includes a variety of meditations that I use with my students. Each meditation has a place where we anchor our attention. These anchors include the breath, sound or phrase (mantra), image, and movement.

Posture is important in any meditation; our body should be sitting upright on a chair or a pillow. Our spine should be straight without being tense. Our eyes can be closed or half-open with a soft gaze.

Observing the Breath

This meditation usually starts with an awareness of the flow of the breath. One follows the breath coming in and out of the nostrils or the rising and falling of the abdomen. We can label the flow of the breath as 'in and out' for the nostrils or 'rising and falling' for the abdomen. Although the breath is the anchor to which we can always return, the awareness can shift to what happens in the moment. For example, the awareness can also focus on the sensations that may arise in the body. If our knee starts to hurt, or our arm itches, the attention can shift to these sensations. The mind simply notices these sensations as they arise and stays focused on them and then notices them pass away. Another area that we can focus on are the feelings that can arise during meditation. For example, if we have had an argument with a colleague, we can be filled with feelings of anger. These feelings can sometimes be very powerful and take over, so we lose our basic awareness of what is happening. Here we can come back to the breath to gain our balance and then return to an awareness of the anger.

Our mind is filled with thoughts, and again we can be taken over by them. For example, thoughts relating to our work can be quite strong; during our meditation we simply try to stay aware of these thoughts. One technique for watching our thoughts is to see them as clouds floating by. Another technique is to label the thoughts. At a general level we can label all thoughts as 'thinking,' or we can be more specific and label the nature of the thoughts. For example, we can use labels like planning, remembering, or imagining. Suzuki Roshi gives some helpful advice for observing our thoughts. They relate to the metaphor of 'big mind' discussed earlier:

> When you are practicing Zazen meditation do not try to stop your thinking. Let it stop by itself. If something comes into your mind, let it come in and let it go out. It will not stay long. When you try to stop your thinking, it means you are bothered by it. Do not be bothered by anything. It appears that the something comes from outside your mind, but actually it is only the waves of your mind and if you are not bothered by the waves, gradually they will become calmer and calmer … If you leave your mind as it is, it will become calm. This mind is called big mind. (cited in Goldstein, 1975, p. 28)

In meditation we are not trying to 'clear the mind' or create some model of what the mind should be. Instead, we are simply being present to what is happening.

If my mind becomes too unsettled by all this, I simply return to the breath. Gradually, however, this meditation allows me to live in the present moment. It allows our natural awareness to arise so that we are not encumbered by our thoughts and feelings. We experience more fully each moment rather than living in the past or projecting ourselves into the future. We gradually learn that all we really have to experience is what is happening right now.

Counting the Breath

Instead of simply observing the breath, we count the exhalations. For example, we can count up to four exhalations and then return to one. Of course, we sometimes get lost in thoughts and go beyond the number four. Eventually we will become aware of this and return to the number one. We do this in a gentle and non-judgmental manner; there is no reproof. We watch ourselves compassionately, and through this process we learn to be compassionate towards others. In both the breath meditations we do not try to control the breath in anyway; we just let the breath do its thing and work from there.

Body Scan

The body is also an excellent anchor for meditation practice and helps us move away from being just in our heads. Also called body sweeping, this technique has been taught by Jon Kabat-Zinn and S.N. Goenka. Kabat-Zinn describes his approach in *Full Catastrophe Living* (1990) while Goenka elaborates on the body scan in his book, *Vipassana Meditation* (1982). The technique starts either at the top of the head or the toes and gradually moves through the entire body. The following are some basic instructions:

Begin by focusing the attention at the top of the head. Note any sensations there. Do you notice any pulsing, itching, or tightness, or is there no particular sensation that arises? Now move the attention to the back of the head. Again be aware of any sensations there. If there is a sensation, focus on that for the moment. Now shift the attention to the left side of the head and then the right side. What sensations do you notice there? Now focus on the face. Be aware of any sensations that arise around the eyes, nose, or mouth.

Now focus on the front of the neck and then gradually move to the sides of the neck and finally the back of the neck. Now gradually move the attention down the back. First, focus on the shoulders and then gradually move to the top of the back. Move slowly down the back noticing any sensation. Tension can be held in the shoulders and the back, so move slowly through this area of the body noting any tightness or pain. If there is any pain, try not to react to the pain but just notice it a non-judgmental manner. Soften the attention where is there is pain or tightness.

Shift the awareness now to the arms. Move the attention down one arm until you reach the hands and the fingers. Again note any sensation or lack thereof. Now move the awareness to the other arm moving the attention down from the shoulder to the hands and fingers.

Focus the attention on the right pelvis area. Now slowly move the awareness down the leg. Focus on the thigh, then the knee. Next scan the lower leg and finally the feet and toes. Shift the attention to the left pelvis area and then move down the leg to the foot and toes noting any sensation that arises. Rest the attention on the feet and toes for a moment.

Now move the awareness back up the body starting with toes and feet and moving through each part again. After moving through the body slowly, you can follow with body scans that are faster as you sweep up and down. The body scan can take as long forty-five minutes.

Mantra

Mantra is the use of a word or phrase as the anchor of awareness. It is repeated over and over in silent sitting meditation or as we do our daily activities. The word mantra comes from the roots *man*, 'the mind,' and *tri*, 'to cross.' Easwaran (1977) states that 'the mantram is that which enables us to cross the sea of the mind' (p. 43).

Mantras exist in almost all religions. The 'Hail Mary' used in Catholicism is a Christian mantra. In Judaism the phrase *Barukh, attah Adonai* means 'Blessed art thou, O Lord' (Easwaran, 1977, p. 60). In the Muslim faith the mantra *Bismillah ir-Rahman ir-Rahim* means 'In the name of Allah, the merciful, the compassionate' (Easwaran, 1977, p. 61). Transcendental meditation, a popular form of meditation, uses a mantra. We can also do a mantra with no religious connection. Herbert Benson (1976) developed the relaxation response, which asks the person to repeat the number one. We can also make up our own mantra by using a word (e.g., peace) or phrase that helps us relax and be present.

Once you have selected a mantra that seems to resonate with you, stick with it. Do not shift mantras during meditation practice. It is also wise not to repeat your mantra to individuals who are not sympathetic to meditation practice. The mantra should not necessarily be a secret, but you want to be able to approach meditation practice with a positive frame of mind.

Having chosen a mantra, you can begin the practice. It is best to begin with your eyes open and to repeat the mantra out loud. Once you have sense of the sound and the rhythm, you can begin to repeat it silently to yourself with your eyes closed or half-open. As you repeat the mantra, get the feeling that the mantra is autonomous; that is, it is repeating itself. You are doing the mantra, but it is going on within you.

> That is all there is to meditating – just sitting peacefully, hearing the mantra in your mind, allowing it to change any way it wants – to get louder or softer – to disappear or return – to stretch out or speed up … Meditation is like drifting on a stream in a boat without oars – because you need no oars – you are not going anywhere. (Carrington, 1977, p. 80)

It is also possible to repeat your mantra during the day. For example, the mantra can be repeated while riding the bus or subway. At work, if you begin to feel tense, you can work with the mantra to deal with the tension. Recently I was giving a presentation at a UNESCO conference and was feeling a little nervous and I repeated the mantra 'I rest in the spirit,' which helped me relax.

You can also use the mantra when you are walking; the mantra can provide a silent rhythm to your walk. Other opportunities for using mantra include times when you are sick or bored. Occasionally we are presented with long stretches of time when there is nothing to do. A good time for mantra is when you lie awake at night. Instead of letting the random thoughts take over, which can often contribute to our restlessness at night, try repeating a mantra. The silent rhythm will focus your mind and may help you return to sleep.

There are times when it is not appropriate to do mantra. For example, if you are doing any job or task which requires your full attention such as driving or listening to music the mantra will be an interference.

Visualization

Visualization was described in chapter 4 as a part of the whole curriculum. Imagery can also be a source of inner growth for teachers. An image in our mind can have powerful effects; for example, if I am afraid of public speaking the image of seeing myself in front of an audience can make my heart beat faster. Guided imagery, or visualization, attempts to elicit images that can foster positive growth and awareness.

Visualization can bring about specific physiological changes. Studies have shown that when an individual imagines himself or herself running, small contractions take place in the muscles associated with running.

We also know that emotional changes can take place through visualization. For example, if we fear flying in an airplane, the image of this event can trigger fear and the accompanying physiological changes. Similarly, a relaxing image, such as walking in a meadow, can lead to a lower heart rate, lower blood pressure, and relaxed muscles. Murphy (1992) states that 'studies have shown that imagery practice can facilitate relief from various afflictions, among them depression, anxiety, insomnia, obesity, sexual problems, chronic pain, phobias, psychosomatic illnesses, cancer, and other diseases' (p. 372).

A simple visualization exercise to begin with is one in which you visualize an object, such as an orange: Set an orange about two or three feet in front of you. Place the orange so that there are no other objects around it to distract your attention ... Relax and breathe deeply ... Now study the orange, notice its shape, colour, and any unusual markings, etc. ... Now close your eyes ... See the image of the orange, for example, the shape, colour and any markings ... Now open your eyes and look at the orange. Compare it with the image you saw. Notice any differences. Now close your eyes and repeat the exercise.

If you have difficulty with this exercise, or with any other, you can come back to it at another time. You may find that images come easier the next time. Piero Ferruci (1982) in his book *What We May Be* presents several visualizations. Here is one called the Fount:

> Imagine a fount springing from granite rock. You see its pure water sparkle in the sun and hear its splashes in the surrounding silence. You experience this special place, where everything is clearer, purer, and more essential.
>
> Start drinking the water, and feel its beneficent energy pervading you and making you feel lighter.
>
> Now walk into the spring itself, letting the water flow over you. Imagine that it has the power of flowing through each one of your body cells and in between them. Imagine it also flowing through the innumerable nuances of your sentiments and emotions, and through your intellect as well. Feel this water cleansing you of all the psychic debris we inevitably accumulate day after day – frustrations, regrets, worries, thoughts of all kinds.
>
> Gradually you experience how the purity of this fount becomes your purity and its energy becomes your energy.
>
> Finally, imagine that you are the fount itself, where all is possible and life is forever new. (p. 123)

The Fount uses water as the central image and symbol. Symbols are integral to the visualization process. Some common symbols found in fantasies and their possible meanings include:

Water: receptivity, passivity, calm
Ascent: growth, inward journey
Cross: tree of life, spiritual connectedness
Hill or mountain: aims or ambitions
Light: creativity, unity, spiritual source
Sun: life force, healing spiritual wholeness (Samuels & Samuels, 1975, p. 97)

A symbol can have many meanings, but we should not get too involved in interpreting them. However, if a symbol is persistent you may want to work with it in meditation or other visualizations in order to see its meaning. One of the best books on visualization is *Seeing with the Mind's Eye: The history, techniques and uses of visualization* by Samuels and Samuels. This book contains a number of visualizations that can be applied to being more creative, dealing with illness, or simply tapping our spiritual natures.

If we feel a connection to a particular person, then we can visualize the presence of that person. We can imagine the love and compassion flowing from that person into our own hearts. Visualizing the presence of another person is called *kything*. Savary and Berne (1988) define kything as a conscious act of spiritual presence. One example of kything that they cite is from Vicktor Frankl's book *Man's Search for Meaning* (1992). One of the ways that Frankl survived in a concentration camp was to imagine the presence of his wife:

> As my friend and I stumbled on for miles, slipping on icy spots, supporting each other time and time again, dragging one another up and onward, nothing was said but we both knew; each of us was thinking of his wife. Occasionally I looked at the sky, where the stars were fading and the pink light of the morning was beginning to spread behind a dark bank of clouds. But my mind clung to my wife's image, imagining it with an uncanny acuteness. I heard her answering me, saw her smile, her frank and encouraging look. Real or not, her look was then more luminous than the sun which was beginning to rise. (p. 68)

Frankl's experience demonstrates the power of visualization as it helped him survive the terrible ordeal of the concentration camp. Sometimes visualization is seen as just a new age technique, but Frankl's example shows the ultimate power of this practice.

Savary and Berne talk about three modes of presence – physical, psychological, and spiritual. Physical presence is simply being together in the same physical space, while psychological presence involves mind-to-mind communication. Kything at the spiritual level can be described as communion.

Movement Meditation

Movement meditations can range from simple walking meditation to yoga or tai chi. Here I briefly describe walking meditation. This meditation is often done in retreats in conjunction with sitting meditation (e.g., insight meditation). For example, the retreat participants alternate between forty-five minutes of sitting meditation and forty-five minutes of walking meditation.

Start with your eyes looking down a few feet ahead of you. Stand for a few moments, being aware of your body standing. Let the arms rest at the side. Now focus on your feet. Feel them supporting you and resting on the ground. The attention in this meditation is on the foot as it touches the ground and moves. The foot, then, is the anchor in this exercise. Slowly lift the foot and gradually place it on the ground.

Walk a short distance forward (e.g., ten or fifteen yards) and then turn around. As you turn, stop for a moment before you resume walking.

It also possible to label the movements; for example, as you lift the foot you might say to yourself 'lifting,' then 'moving' as you move it and 'touching' as it touches the ground again. However, the important thing is to keep the attention focused on the feet and the movements.

At the end of the meditation you can stand for a few moments and simply be aware of your entire body.

Getting Started

If you have never meditated before, you may want to try different methods until you find the one you are most comfortable with. Once you have settled on an approach, stick with it. If you keep changing, your practice will never deepen.

To begin stationary meditation practice, sit comfortably with your head, neck, and chest in a straight line. You can sit in a chair or cross-legged on a cushion or bench. Most importantly, you should be in a position where you will not be shifting around a lot during the meditation.

It is probably best to meditate at least one hour after eating. The times that seem to be most popular for meditation are early in the morning upon arising or in the evening. You should choose a place free of distractions. If you have a room for meditation, fine; if not, then a corner of a bedroom can also be arranged so that it is conducive to meditation. Once you have settled on a time and place, others in the household should be made aware that you are not to be disturbed unless there is something urgent. However, you should not be unreasonable about your practice. For example, if there are young children in the household you should probably not choose to meditate right before dinner, as this is usually a busy time and meditation practice could interfere with the needs of the family. Meditation should be done so that family life patterns are not drastically disturbed.

A period of twenty minutes is appropriate to begin meditation practice. As you commit yourself to a particular method, then you can lengthen the period to thirty or forty minutes. During meditation it is perfectly all right to check your watch or a clock; timers are also available. At the end remain seated for a minute or two, thus allowing a space between the meditation and the resumption of daily activities.

References

Benson, H. (1976). *The relaxation response.* New York: Avon.

Carrington, P. (1977). *Freedom in meditation.* New York: Doubleday.

Easwaran, E. (1977). *The mantram handbook: Formulas for transformation.* Berkeley, CA: Nilgri Press.

Ferruci, P. (1982) *What we may be: Techniques for psychological and spiritual growth.* Los Angeles, CA: Tarcher.

Frankl, V. (1992). *Man's search for meaning.* Boston: Beacon.

Goenka, S.N. (1982). *Vipassana meditation.* New York: Harper and Row.

Goldstein, J. (1975). *The experience of insight: A natural unfolding.* Santa Cruz, CA: Unity Press.

Kabat-Zinn, J. (1990). *Full catastrophe living: Using the wisdom of your body and mind to face stress, pain and illness.* New York: Delacorte Press.

Murphy, M. (1992). *The future of the body: Explorations into the further evolution of human nature.* New York: Jeremy Tarcher.

Samuels, M., & Samuels, N. (1975) *Seeing with the mind's eye: The history, techniques and uses of visualization.* New York: Random House.

Savary, L.M., & Berne, P.H. (1988). *Kything: The art of spiritual presence.* Mahwah, NJ: Paulist Press.

Index